# FATHER ME

———•———

## GLENN DORSEY

Copyright © 2014 Glenn Dorsey
All rights reserved.

ISBN: 1500534293
ISBN 13: 9781500534295
Library of Congress Control Number: 2014913027
CreateSpace Independent Publishing Platform, North Charleston, SouthCarolina

Unless otherwise indicated, all Scripture is taken from The Holy Bible, English Standard Version. Copyright © 2001 by Crossway Bibles, a division of Good News Publishers.

Scripture marked KJV is taken from the King James Version of the Bible.

Scripture marked NIV is taken from the Holy Bible, New International Version®, NIV® Copyright © 1973, 1978, 1984, 2011 by Biblica, Inc.® Used by permission. All rights reserved worldwide.

Scripture marked NKJV is taken from The Holy Bible, New King James Version. Copyright © 1982 by Thomas Nelson, Inc.

Scripture marked NLT is taken from the Holy Bible. New Living Translation. Copyright © 1996, 2004, 2007, 2013 by Tyndale House Foundation. Used by permission of Tyndale House Publishers Inc., Carol Stream, Illinois 60188. All rights reserved.

This book is dedicated in memory of my loving father, Rev. Buford Dorsey.
He was not a perfect man but was a perfect father.
Because of him I have a healthy concept of Father God.

# Contents

Preface . . . . . . . . . . . . . . . . . . . . . . . . . . . . . . . . . . . . . . . . . . . . . . . . . . . . . . . vii

Chapter 1: Where Is Your Father? . . . . . . . . . . . . . . . . . . . . . . . . . . . . . . . . . 1

Chapter 2: Our Father . . . . . . . . . . . . . . . . . . . . . . . . . . . . . . . . . . . . . . . . . . 17

Chapter 3: How to Honor a Father You Don't Respect . . . . . . . . . . . . . . . . . 27

Chapter 4: Give Me Your Presence . . . . . . . . . . . . . . . . . . . . . . . . . . . . . . . . 39

Chapter 5: I Want to Be "So Loved" . . . . . . . . . . . . . . . . . . . . . . . . . . . . . . . 49

Chapter 6: Protect Me . . . . . . . . . . . . . . . . . . . . . . . . . . . . . . . . . . . . . . . . . 69

Chapter 7: I Want Your Instruction . . . . . . . . . . . . . . . . . . . . . . . . . . . . . . . 81

Chapter 8: How Do I Remain Sexually Pure? . . . . . . . . . . . . . . . . . . . . . . . 95

Chapter 9: Will You Give Me a Father's Blessing? . . . . . . . . . . . . . . . . . . . 109

Chapter 10: Prepare Me to Live Independently of You . . . . . . . . . . . . . . . . 119

Conclusion . . . . . . . . . . . . . . . . . . . . . . . . . . . . . . . . . . . . . . . . . . . . . . . . 135

# Preface

**H**AVING TRAVELED THE WORLD WITH THE GOSPEL message of emotional healing, I have discovered that the relative health of a society is determined mostly by the success or failure of its fathers in the home.

America is in a social crisis because the home is being attacked by new definitions of what constitutes a family.

This book speaks to fathers about the needs of their children and about how to become better fathers. It is also intended to speak to the fatherless, who indeed have a Heavenly Father who desires a genuine relationship with them.

How does a fatherless son know how to be a father? He will struggle, at best. Virgil Foster was my brother-in-law. When he was a small boy, his father abandoned the family. Finally, after many years, after Virgil had adult children himself, his father reappeared. He wanted forgiveness and to develop a relationship with him.

Virgil was not a man of much emotion, but as he shared his exasperation with me, I could feel the frustration and pain in his voice. He said, "He wasn't there when I needed a father. I became a father, and things that should have come naturally to me were a struggle because I had no father image in my life. I didn't know what a father was supposed to do with his children."

Thank God that He has given us hope that, in the latter days, a restoration is coming between fathers and sons. The last prophecy given in the Old Testament is about the desire of God to restore the relationship of fathers and sons.

*Malachi 4:6:* "And he will turn the hearts of fathers to their children and the hearts of children to their fathers, lest I come and strike the land with a decree of utter destruction."

This promise to restore father-son relationships strongly implies that the hearts of fathers have turned away, and thus the hearts of the sons have turned away as well. Countless times, in an emotional healing interview, I have heard the deep pain of a person who has been rejected, abused, violated, or traumatized in some way by a father. Sadly, many of these fathers said they were Christians.

It is my desire that this book will give insight to fathers concerning the heart cry of their children for what they want and need from a father. America is being cursed because of the absence of fathers in the home. The majority of the youth in America are seeking father figures who will become their role models.

Fathers, no one can take your place. May the Father, and all fathers, respond to the needy cry of the next generation: "Father me!"

Chapter 1

# WHERE IS YOUR FATHER?

> *"It is easier for a father to have children than for children to have a real father."*
> —*Pope John XXIII*

**MOST EVERY MAN CAN FATHER A CHILD,** but not every man who fathers a child becomes a father.

What would our world be like without fathers' being present? Many in America fully understand that situation. They are fatherless, or their fathers are emotionally disconnected from them. A part of their lives is missing because their father has not been there for them. The greatest missing part of that relationship is establishing their identity.

Those who questioned Jesus' identity asked Him a question that today many can identify with as well.

*John 8:19:* "They said to him therefore, 'Where is your Father?'"

# FATHER ME

When my daughter Lisa was in elementary school, she came home crying one day. I asked her why she was crying, and she said, "The kids at school are calling me a liar."

"Why are they calling you a liar?" I asked.

"They asked me if I had both of my original parents at home, and I answered yes, Daddy!" she exclaimed. "They wouldn't believe me. I am the only one in my class that has their real parents!"

That day I came to a shocking realization of the dilemma that will affect the future morality and stability of the American family. I have lived long enough to see the results of divorce and the pain that comes from the absence of fathers.

Perhaps you can relate to the following quotes by two famous people:

> *"When I was a youngster, I lived with different families. I nearly always felt closer to the man of the house. Maybe because I always dreamed of having a father of my own."*
> —Marilyn Monroe
>
> *"My father? I never knew him. Never even seen a picture of him."*
> —Eminem

"Where is your father?" is a very emotional, embarrassing, and challenging question for a person to be asked if his or her father is absent. Often it will be answered with a lame excuse or outright lie because they do not want others to know the true reason their father is not present.

There are four basic reasons why a living father may not be present.

## ILLEGITIMACY

Is America becoming like Ashdod? Ashdod is a place in the Bible that was known for illegitimate children.

*Zechariah 9:6 (KJV):* "A bastard [illegitimate; *mamzer* in Hebrew] shall dwell in Ashdod."

Illegitimate births are on the rise in America, for various reasons. In 2010 the National Center for Health Statistics reported the following:

- Number of births in the United States: 4,316,233
- Number of live births to unmarried women: 1,715,047
- Percent unmarried: 40%

Almost half of the babies being born in America are being raised in single-parent homes. We are experiencing a generation that is being raised without fathers and without the traditional parental set of mother and father. Couples are living together without marriage, and the father figure becomes confusing because it may change frequently with a new face in the house.

The illegitimate child will struggle with acceptance. Too often they are rejected by both of their parents. Their parents go on with their lives, creating families where the illegitimate child is often neglected emotionally and treated as though he or she does not exist.

One of the people on my heroes list is Liz Jones. She is a petite, neat, refined, and articulate person. To look at her, you would never discern the pain of her past. She is on my heroes list because of what she has overcome.

This is her story.

Liz was the product of a one-night stand. Her mother was a teenager. Her father, in his early twenties, came from a conservative religious background. Neither of her parents was prepared to take responsibility for her. Due to these circumstances, Liz would be raised in the home of her grandmother.

She knew who her father was, and he knew who she was. Her father married and had other children. Her mother married and did the same. Liz suffered from the absence of both her father and her mother.

She longed to be with her father, to talk with him, but her father's wife did not want her to interfere with their family. So Liz was not allowed to attend family reunions or family gatherings. Such rejection! Liz lived her childhood longing for the time she could be with her father. Her family continued to treat her as an outcast or outsider even into her adult life.

Liz went on with her life. She eventually married, educated herself, and became an outstanding high school counselor. Her personal concern and love touched the hearts of many students through the years until she retired. She had the unique ability to identify with children who were neglected or who were struggling with family issues, and she gave them wise counsel.

But there was one special window of time—one uninterrupted hour—that Liz would have as a married woman with her father. He had contracted cancer and would live only a year after this special meeting. But in the hour of time that she had with her father, Liz was able to receive everything that she had longed for. With tear-filled eyes, she shared with me that her father had told her that he loved her, that he had kept up with what had been going on in her life, and that he was proud of her. He shared with her that he would have had more contact with her, but it would have created major problems with his wife.

I share this story because the most important time in Liz's life was that single hour that she was able to be with her father! That was a tremendous, healing moment for her. When she was privileged to hear the words "I love you," she was able to go on with her life.

Her father died, and the only person who had recognized her as a family member told her that because of the circumstances, she was not invited to attend her father's funeral, again because of his wife. It was the ultimate rejection. It would have completely annihilated any sense of self-worth in the average person. But not Liz. She had received her identity in that one hour with her dad.

What a woman of courage and personal strength. She has found her complete identity in Father God. The Father has affirmed her and given her grace to minister to others who are living with emotional pain in their lives.

## Divorce

God hates divorce because of the pain and disorder it brings to those affected by it.

A younger couple was having a heated argument that awakened their son from his sleep. Unaware that he was standing in the doorway, they continued degrading and putting blame on each other. Finally the man screamed, "I can't think of one reason why I should stay in this marriage!" Before he could continue, his son cried out and said, "Daddy, could I be that reason?"

Recently, a child made a statement to me in conversation that caused me to understand how divorce affects a child. He said, "When *we* divorced." Suddenly I was made aware of the fact that it is not just a father and mother divorcing; it is also the divorcing of the children.

"We have too many full-time children in America with part-time parents." What a truth!

I have known several instances where fathers have divorced, remarried, and started another family. They told the children from the first marriage to forget they had a father. They said they never wanted to see those children again.

In one particular case, some of the children attempted to pursue a relationship with their father several years after the divorce. They showed up at his door unexpectedly. They were certain that he would be glad to see them. He responded by saying, "I don't know you. You are not my children." They said, "No! You are our father. You named us!" He again said, "I don't know you. Please leave."

The emotional pain and trauma is overwhelming in such cases. Children often blame themselves for causing the divorce. Their role of son or daughter may change to being a caregiver of a parent or becoming a parent to their siblings. They may blame themselves for the lack of finances in the home.

**Physical Absence**

The physical absence of a father in the home also creates behavioral and social issues. Society is affected by the absence of a father in the home.

The following statistics give proof to the impact of fatherless homes:

- **63%** of **youth suicides** are from fatherless homes. (Source: USDHHS, Bureau of the Census)
- **90%** of all **homeless and runaway children** are from fatherless homes. (Source: USDHHS, Bureau of the Census)
- **85%** of all children that exhibit **behavioral disorders** come from fatherless homes. (Source: Centers for Disease Control)
- **80%** of **rapists** motivated with displaced anger come from fatherless homes. (Source: *Criminal Justice & Behavior*, Vol. 14, pp. 403–26, 1978)

- **71%** of all **high school dropouts** come from fatherless homes. (Source: National Principals Association Report on the State of High Schools)
- **75%** of all **adolescent patients in chemical abuse centers** come from fatherless homes. (Source: *Rainbows for All God's Children*)
- **70%** of **juveniles in state-operated institutions** come from fatherless homes. Source: US Department of Justice, Special Report, September 1988)

These statistics mean that children from a fatherless home are:

- Five times more likely to commit suicide.
- Thirty-two times more likely to run away.
- Twenty times more likely to have behavioral disorders.
- Fourteen times more likely to commit rape.
- Nine times more likely to drop out of high school.
- Ten times more likely to abuse chemical substances.
- Nine times more likely to end up in a state-operated institution.
- Twenty times more likely to end up in prison.

**Confused Identities.** Boys who grow up in father-absent homes are more likely than those in father-present homes to have trouble establishing appropriate sex roles and gender identity. (P.L. Adams, J.R. Milner, and N.A. Schrepf, *Fatherless Children*, New York, Wiley Press, 1984.)

**Aggression.** In a longitudinal study of 1,197 fourth-grade students, researchers observed "greater levels of aggression in boys from mother-only households than from boys in mother-father households." (N. Vaden-Kierman, N. Ialongo, J. Pearson, and S. Kellam, "Household Family Structure and Children's Aggressive Behavior: A Longitudinal Study of Urban Elementary School Children," *Journal of Abnormal Child Psychology* 23, no. 5, 1995.)

Fathers, you are irreplaceable. You are the cornerstone of our society.

## Emotional Abandonment

Almost weekly, I deal with people who have been wounded in their past, either by a father who was physically in the home but emotionally disconnected from the family, or by a father who was absent much of the time.

Too many men, whether deliberately or unconsciously, use their job to escape the responsibilities of being a father. They ease their conscience by saying, "A man must be a provider," or "I have to work this second job to make ends meet." Is the sole purpose or function of a father to a family to be a provider? Could it be that there is a much deeper reason than even they themselves discern? *Could it be that they do not know how to be fathers?*

The father who is emotionally absent sends an obvious message to the child that other people or things are more important to him than the child. Too often, I hear statements such as these:

- My father was never at my games.
- My father was never there when I needed him.
- My father was a drill sergeant. He came home, gave orders, and disappeared.
- My father was never home. He was always at work.
- My father spent more time with the dogs than he did with me.

Children interpret time spent with them as importance being placed upon them. Our children long to be with us. It saddens me to see a father push his clinging children away as if they are an irritation. The very reason they are clinging is because they are not getting enough attention.

To grow up in a home with a father you don't know is a painful experience. Children's minds are filled with many questions about their dads that demand answers:

- Why does he never share with me any of his family history?
- Why does he never speak about his father?
- Why does he never ask me how I am doing in school?
- Why does he never ask me who won the game?
- Why does he never take me fishing or hunting or play games with me?

Children who have been separated from their father's presence because of death, divorce, separation, adoption, illegitimacy, or rape face many issues that deeply affect their identities.

There's another question that may be even more troubling than where a person's father is, and that is, "*Who* is your father?" Regardless of the circumstances, a person who does not know who his or her father is will struggle with identity. These issues raise questions and thoughts that are accusatory, and they create emotions that are difficult to deal with. They include:

- **Rejection**
  Why can't I have both parents?
  You can't live with us; you aren't one of us.

- **Lack of identity**
  Who am I?
  You don't know who your father/mother is?

- **Displaced**
  Where do I belong?
  Where is home?
  Which man do I call my father?

- **Unwanted**
  You are somebody's mistake!

- **Lesser or inferior**
  I am the black sheep.
  I am never treated the same as others in the family.

Often I tell my congregation that I am preaching to people of greater faith than I possess. What I mean is that they have had ominous personal challenges in life that I have never experienced, and they have overcome them. The people who possess the strongest faith have also faced the most difficult circumstances.

Outwardly, many of them show no signs of the emotional pain they have suffered. Some people might have become angry with God and themselves. And others might have turned to bad relationships, drugs, or addictive behaviors to ease the pain. Yet these people and their families are in the house of God with hands raised, worshiping the God of grace.

One Sunday morning during my sermon, I called out of the congregation people who were on my heroes list and asked them to come to the front of the sanctuary so they could tell their stories. Leah Smith was one of them.

A person of another race raped Leah's mother. She was the product of that rape. Her mother's husband became the only father she would know. He raised her and accepted her as his own. Her family suffered many traumas. Her brother was murdered; other siblings had issues with drugs; and her father suffered trauma to his brain from boxing while he was in the military.

Through all of this, Leah's mother and father raised her to serve the Lord. I observed her through most of her childhood as she grew into the outstanding young lady she is today. She struggled with her identity. She struggled with her racial identity.

But Leah made a choice to claim her identity with God the Father. Out of that relationship, she has become one of the most gifted songwriters and worship leaders that I know. She is a gifted photographer and graphic designer. She has convinced me that she can do anything. She is living proof that God the Father can take a nightmare and turn it into a dream. Today Leah has great dreams and visions for how God will use her. He will fulfill her dreams above her expectations.

There is hope for the fatherless. God has promised that He will be a "Father of the fatherless" (Psalm 68:5).

I heard a story told that reinforces this truth.

A boy was born to an unwed mother who lived in a small town in the mountains of Tennessee. Throughout his childhood he would be asked the same question, "Who's your daddy?" It would be asked innocently, other times intentionally. He dreaded that question being asked. He lived with the pain of not knowing who his father was.

He would go to great lengths to avoid people as much as possible to avoid that question being asked. He would often miss school or if he were there would hide from the other children.

A new pastor came to the church he attended when he was twelve. He asked Ben, "Son, who is your daddy?" Immediately the pastor detected that he had asked the boy a question that made him uncomfortable. He continued by saying, "I should have known. I see the family resemblance. You are a child of God. You have a great future in front of you."

When Ben would be asked that question from then on his response would be, "I am a child of God."

This young man, Ben, would later become Ben Hooper, the governor of Tennessee.

The church becomes like family to the believer, because we share the fatherhood of God. This truth is exemplified by the testimony of Dan Nemlowill.

Dan was a young man who began attending our church as a college student. Because his stepfather was in the military, the family moved often, and each time Dan had to make new friends. When he was eighteen, his mother informed Dan that she was leaving his stepfather; that he was on his own; and that they must go their separate ways.

Father's Day and Christmas were two of Dan's worst holidays. It was difficult and awkward for him to receive gifts or to be celebrated. We gave him a surprise birthday party, thinking it would be an encouragement to him and make him feel like family. Instead, it made him very uncomfortable. I discovered later that it was the first time in his life that he had been given a birthday celebration.

Shortly after becoming a believer, Dan was baptized in water. As a part of his testimony he said, "I did not know what family was until I started coming to this church." Thank God for churches that have this effect on those who worship with them.

Dan became a part of our church family. After giving his life to Christ, he received the baptism in the Holy Spirit and was called into the ministry. Dan graduated from Central Bible College in Springfield, Missouri. He is now married to a wonderful woman of God. Dan also has served as a youth pastor, associate pastor, and pastor of a church.

Dan was never given much information about his biological father, but he had a need that only his father could meet. He wanted to learn something about his family history. He would go through a miraculous turn of events in the quest of searching for his father.

## WHERE IS YOUR FATHER?

As a young man, Dan had gone to the home of the man he thought was his father and announced himself. The man who answered the door said, "Get out of my face! I never want to see you again." Of course, this was an overwhelming rejection that wounded Dan's spirit for a long time.

Later in his ministry, Dan felt led by the Lord to attempt to contact his father again. He Googled his father's name and discovered that he was a doctor who lived in a western coastal state. Dan made contact with him, and they set up a meeting to become acquainted.

Dan learned that his parents had gotten married while his father was a medical student, because his mother was pregnant. The marriage was rocky, and due to several issues, they soon broke up. Dan had been too young to have any real memories of his father. But then his father told him, "Dan, I always wanted you. I got you every other weekend, but suddenly your mother and you were gone. I never knew what happened to you."

Can you imagine the emotions Dan felt when he learned that his father had actually wanted him? The man Dan had first contacted, the one he thought was his father, was not. He was a family member, but not Dan's father.

During the time Dan spent with his father, he learned many things about himself and his father that he had not known. His life changed when the blanks were filled in about his past and who his father was.

We all have a common need to know our father. Whether you were conceived by rape, an illegitimate relationship, a teenage pregnancy, or in a healthy marriage relationship, you desire to know your father.

You may have been adopted by a wonderful family, abandoned early in your life, or your father may have died before you were old enough to remember him—regardless of your circumstances, you have a desire to know something about your father.

In the quest to discover who our father is, we can trace the roots of our family trees, and this will lead us all to the Father of fathers.

Luke 3:23–38 tells us about the lineage of Joseph, who was married to Mary, the mother of Jesus. Luke's story takes us all the way back to Adam. The lineage ends with these words: "The son of Adam, the son of God."

This Scripture makes it clear that we are the children of God. We are made in His image and likeness. Does this not describe a father and child relationship? How many times have you heard someone say, "You are the spitting image of your father"?

God's relationship with Adam was as a father to his son. He gave Adam His likeness, image, presence, focus, work ethic, a name, a life plan, words of affirmation, and dominion over all the earth.

When Jesus came to earth, He came with the revelation of God as the Father.

*John 14:9:* "Jesus said to him, 'Whoever has seen me has seen the Father. How can you say, "Show us the Father?"'"

Christianity is the only religion in the world that calls God "Father." We have a Heavenly Father! We will understand His importance in our life in the next chapter.

## DISCUSSION QUESTIONS

1. How would you describe your relationship with your father?

2. What are four basic reasons a living father is not present with his children?

3. What are some emotions a child experiences when a father is deliberately absent from the child's life?

4. In what way does the father not being in the home affect society? What do statistics reflect about this issue?

5. How much time do you spend individually with your children each day?

Chapter 2

# OUR FATHER

When Jesus wanted us to understand our relationship with God, He used a word of endearment: Father. He said, "When you pray, say 'Our Father which art in heaven.'" He could have said to address God with Old Testament names such as Yahweh or Jehovah. These names had variations that referred to His character. These names seem to put God at a distance. They make Him seem unapproachable. Instead Jesus chose to use the word *Father* under the New Covenant, to give us the true revelation of God and His love for us.

Jesus did not say, "When you pray, say *my* Father." He said to pray, "Our Father." God is not just the father of Jesus. He is *our* Father. He belongs to all of us. We are His children!

The word *father* carries with it many emotions determined by the relationship you have had with your natural father. It may create fear, anger, love, affection, emptiness, or abandonment.

I was taking a young lady through an emotional healing process. She was distraught about the word *father*. The Holy Spirit informed me that when she prayed, she did not call upon Him as Father, but as God. I asked her to say the Lord's Prayer out loud and to call upon God as Father. She broke down and wept. I asked her why she struggled calling upon God as Father. Her response was, "My father molested me!"

The emotions that are attached to the word *father* vary for each of us. Our understanding of God as our Father is closely connected to our relationship with our biological father or father figure.

Unconsciously our children will relate to God in the same manner that they relate to us. Proverbs 17:6 says that "the glory of children is their fathers." Whatever our earthly father has not been to us, our Heavenly Father will be. We have a Heavenly Father who is the perfect father. We can glory in Him!

An assignment was given to my high school literature class to write an essay about the person we most admired. I thought to myself, "This is easy. However, everyone will be writing about the same person: their father."

I was quite shocked and disconcerted when the essays were read openly in class. Only I and one other person had written about our fathers. It had never been revealed to me how blessed I was to have such a wonderful father until that moment.

We all assume that everyone's father is like our own.

Why did I choose my father as the most admired person for my essay? My father was not a perfect man, but he was a perfect father. In my early childhood, the more I learned about the struggles my father overcame, the more I respected and admired him.

He was reared in a large farm family. He was introduced to hard physical labor as a child. As the second oldest sibling, he was deprived of a proper education, because he was required to help work on the farm. He did not have the privilege of completing an elementary education. He did not make it past the fifth grade.

His father was an abusive alcoholic. There was a great deal of dysfunction in the home. Because of his father's addiction, Dad did not receive from his father the emotional support that every child seeks and deserves. He had a very poor self-image due to a lack of education and the poverty in which he lived.

A Nazarene preacher, Rev. Houston Johnson, often visited the farm. Many times while my grandfather was drinking, the preacher witnessed to the family about Jesus and how He could change their lives. My father later became a lifetime follower of Jesus Christ. When Dad accepted Jesus Christ into his life, he broke a generational sin from future posterity.

He married my mother and was called into ministry. When my father was in school, he had not been able to focus in class because of the events that were happening in the home. The Holy Spirit taught my father how to read and write.

Whatever my father did not receive from his father, he gave to me. He gave me words of affirmation, love, affection, security, presence, protection, and self-confidence, just to mention a few.

When I discovered the hardships and adversities my father had overcome, and I understood the effort he made in being my father, it created in me a lifetime of respect and admiration.

As children, we want our father to be larger than life. Perhaps we have heard it expressed in the following statements:

- My dad is stronger than your dad!
- My dad can whip your dad!
- My dad can do anything!
- My dad knows everything.

# FATHER ME

My father, to me, was all the above.

> *"I am not ashamed to say that no man I ever met was my father's equal, and I never loved any other man as much."* —Hedy Lamarr

Jesus said of our Father in John 10:29, "My father...is greater than all."

I want to boast about our Father.

- He created all things, visible and invisible, by the word of His mouth. He spoke, and it was so.—*Genesis 1*

- He parted the Red Sea with a blast of His nostrils.—*Exodus 15:8*

- He has measured the waters in the hollow of His hand, marked off the heavens with a span, enclosed the dust of the earth in a measure, and weighed the mountains in scales and the hills in a balance.—*Isaiah 40:12*

- He knows the end from the beginning.—*Isaiah 46:10*

- He knew us before we were in our mother's womb.—*Jeremiah 1:5*

- His love cannot be measured.—*Ephesians 3:18–19*

Our Father is all-powerful, all-knowing, always present, and has always been. He is omnipotent, omniscient, omnipresent, and eternal.

Your children want to see you in the same manner we have just described the Heavenly Father: larger than life!

## OUR FATHER

Because God is our Father, we are to honor Him. He demands it.

*Malachi 1:6:* "A son honors his father, and a servant his master. If then I am a father, where is my honor?"

Our Father commanded us to "honor thy father" in the Ten Commandments. Let's give our children fathers that they will honor. What all children desire and deserve is a father they can respect and admire. You have been given the unique ability to make lifelong deposits in your children that no one else can make. You can make deposits that will give them self-confidence and self-worth.

*God has placed it in the heart of a child to please his father.* Think about that! Fatherhood is intended to be a positive life experience, not a dread.

*Colossians 3:21:* "Fathers, do not provoke [incite or make angry] your children, lest they become discouraged."

Could it be that the reason our children demonstrate anger and frustration is because we are not meeting their needs? Could it be that our children are angry with themselves because they can't do well enough to please us? If so, this may not be a behavioral issue with a child, but a father who is not meeting the emotional needs of the child.

This was true in the life of Michael Jackson. No doubt many of the unusual behaviors of Michael Jackson came from the frustration of his relationship with his father. In more than one interview, he stated that he could never please his father and suggested that he had been the recipient of abuse.

> *"I just wish I could understand my father."*
> —*Michael Jackson*

# FATHER ME

Because God has placed it in the heart of the child to glory in his father, you have the power to create a larger-than-life persona of what a wonderful father is like. In fact, you have the opportunity to reveal to your child the fatherhood of God. What makes a child's father larger than life? It begins with establishing a *relationship* with your child early in his life, and being consistently involved in his daily life.

Wherever my father was, that's where I wanted to be. Whatever he was doing, I wanted to be doing it with him. Whether I was interested in what he was doing at the time or not really did not matter. I was with my dad.

I remember on a frigid winter day, I cried to go hunting with my father. He did not want me to go because I did not have suitable boots to keep my feet warm and dry. Because I continued to cry, he gave in, against his better judgment.

That day became one of the most memorable, miserable, and valued days of my life. Having nothing but sneakers to wear, I lasted but a short time in the snow, water, and freezing temperatures. I could not continue without his helping me to get warm. He took off my shoes and socks, wrung the water out of them, and then blew on my feet till they were warm again. He put my shoes and socks back on my feet, and we continued the hunt. He carried me on his back to keep my feet out of the snow until he became too exhausted to carry me any further. Then I had to walk in the snow, and eventually my feet got cold and wet again. We repeated this process throughout the day.

Through all the misery of adverse weather, being with my dad—carried by him, warmed by him, and sharing that hunt—has become a cherished, lasting memory.

Dad always had time for me. He made life interesting and fun.

## OUR FATHER

Brooks Adams kept a diary as a child. He wrote when he was eight years old, "Today I went fishing with my father, the most glorious day of my life." His dad was ambassador to Britain under President Lincoln.

On the other hand, his father wrote in his diary concerning the same day, "Went fishing with my son, a day wasted."

*Never* think that your time with your child is a waste! Just be present in the time you have together.

We receive our identity from our father. He gives us our name. He tells us who we are and who we are not. Whatever he tells us about ourselves is fixed in our minds, and we will live this out. As a father, the words you speak over your child will set him on a course that you have prescribed for him.

Our Heavenly Father has given us a name! We will receive this name when we are with Jesus in the Father's house.

*Ephesians 3:14–15 (KJV):* "For this cause I bow my knees unto the Father of our Lord Jesus Christ, of whom the whole family in heaven and earth is named."

*Revelation 2:17 (NLT):* "And I will give to each one a white stone, and on the stone will be engraved a new name that no one understands except the one who receives it."

With this new name, we receive a new identity. The names of many people throughout the Bible were changed following an encounter with God. Abram the fatherless became Abraham the father of nations. Sarai the barren became Sarah the mother of nations. Jacob the deceiver became Israel the prince of God. Simon the rock fragment became Peter the rock. And Saul the persecutor became Paul the Apostle.

The stars of the heavens are innumerable, yet God calls each of them by name. He also has a name that is unique and special for you. It is a name that defines and describes your personality as God the Father sees you.

From our Father we receive a new identity that frees us to become all that He desires us to be. Our fulfillment is in Him. We are who our Father says we are. Too long we have been told who we are not! Our Father tells us who we are and who we can become.

One of the first words we learn to speak is *dad*. Just as we, early in our lives, called for our father, the same is true in the spiritual realm. When we are born again, the first words our spirit speaks are evidence of our salvation. And according to Romans 8, the first words our spirit speaks are, "Abba, Father."

*Romans 8:15 (NLT):* "You have not received a spirit that makes you fearful slaves. Instead, you received God's Spirit when he adopted you as his own children. Now we call him, 'Abba, Father.'"

May our goal, as fathers, be to make the word *father* a word that is embraced and honored by our children. Let us do everything within our power to make the word *father* a name that leads our children to *the Father*. As the Heavenly Father has given us an identity, may we as fathers also give our children a blessed identity.

May our goal be to fulfill Proverbs 17:6, "The glory of children is their fathers."

## DISCUSSION QUESTIONS

1. Are you being a father your children can admire?

2. What steps are you taking to give your children knowledge about the real you?

3. Are you creating a special, uninterrupted time to be with each of your children?

4. What identity are you giving your child?

5. What blessings are you bestowing upon your children that you did not receive from your father?

6. What image of God as the Father are you giving your children by your example?

7. What words would your children use to describe the Heavenly Father?

## Chapter 3

# HOW TO HONOR A FATHER YOU DON'T RESPECT

A PERSON WHO HAS A GOOD RELATIONSHIP WITH his father needs no teaching on how to honor his father. It comes to him easily and naturally because of the love he has received from him. However it is no small struggle to honor a father you feel doesn't deserve it. You may feel that by honoring your father you are really excusing his behavior. That is not the case at all.

God our Father demands honor. Malachi 1:6, " If then I am a father, where is my honor?"

We are instructed in the Bible to honor our father. It is not a choice but a command.

*Exodus 20:12:* "Honor your father and your mother, that your days may be long in the land that the Lord your God is giving you."

Those who have fathers that have emotionally or physically abandoned them, physically or sexually abused them, will struggle with the demands of this commandment.

Regardless of the offense one may have experienced by the failures of their father it does not change the instruction God has given. As difficult as it may seem we can fulfill its command.

My father exemplified this with his life. This is part of his story. It is not intended to dishonor my grandfather but to learn a life lesson from my father's relationship to him and how he responded to him. He was a good man unless he was drinking. The only problem was that most of the time he was drinking.

It was not uncommon for my grandfather, while in a drunken condition, to beat my grandmother. When my dad reached his teenage years he could not deal with it anymore.
He felt he had to do something to stop his father. One winter evening he heard his father nearing home singing a gospel song in a drunken state. He hid in a closet with a loaded 22 rifle determined that if his father laid a hand to his mother he would shoot him. Dad said, "It must have been the prayers of my mother, but for some reason that night my dad slept in the yard and didn't come in the house."

Though later he would become an ordained minister and would pastor for several years, I observed the scars that remained and the effects the emotional pain left in his life. The insecurity, the lack of an education, and the lack of self-confidence were issues he would struggle with all his life. They would take an accumulative toll on his life.

At the age of seventy-seven he would experience a nervous breakdown. The psychiatrist informed us that he was fully dealing with the issues of his childhood. The impact of the abuse would follow him to his grave. One of the last conversations that I had with my father he said, "My father treated me worse than a dog."

Though my father experienced such a horrific childhood, as an adult he modeled how one can honor a parent they do not respect.

The obvious question is, "Why should I honor a father I don't respect?"

Dr. Mike Murdock asked, "If you cannot honor the person that is responsible for bringing you into the world how can you honor God that you have not seen?" We did not choose our parents, but guess who did? God, who knows the end from the beginning, knew the home that you would be raised in. God is not responsible for the evil or pain others have imposed in your life. Honor is a choice, a decision we make to obey God's command. We understand that we are honoring God because we choose to honor the person that brought us into the world.

We not only honor God by honoring our father but we also honor God by loving our father. The greatest commandment that supersedes the fifth commandment is the second commandment. Matthew 22:39, "And a second is like it: You shall love your neighbor as yourself."

Love for a hurtful parent doesn't come from our own abilities. It will come by our relationship that we have with God the Father. Through the power of the Holy Spirit we can choose to love those who we feel don't deserve it. When my grandfather died Dad said, " My father was a horrible man, but I loved him."

Now we have answered the question, "*Why* should I honor a father I do not respect?" let's answer the all-important question, "*How* then can I honor a father I do not respect?"

I offer the following suggestions of ways to honor a father you don't respect.

**Teach your children to honor their grandfather by extending mercy to him.**

Speak kindly about him and don't exaggerate his mistakes. Be full of mercy. Yes, the truth must be known. Your children will sympathize with your pain. They may hold a grudge for the pain your father caused you. Because of this we must model mercy before them. We strengthen the family when we teach by example that we all need mercy. Jesus said, "The merciful shall obtain mercy."

Mercy is leniency shown toward offenders. It is not judging and giving them a sentence they deserve. God will do that at the judgment.

There may be a time in your future when you will need mercy.

Do you consider yourself to be a good person? If you said "yes," then allow me to ask you a few questions.
Have you ever told a lie?
Have you ever taken anything that didn't belong to you?
Have you ever lusted?

If the answer to any of those questions is yes, you broke the Ten Commandments just as much as the father who offended you. If we break one commandment we are capable of breaking all of them. We all have sinned and come short of the glory of God. The merciful will obtain mercy.

Your children will honor you because you chose to honor your father.

**Forgive your father's transgressions.**

Your father can say, "I'm sorry," yet the wound remains. When your father fails you there is only one way that healing is going to come into our lives and that is when we take on the attitude of Jesus Christ, and forgive. He gave us the parable in Matthew 18 about a servant who owed his master a debt. The master forgives him of that debt. That servant also had people that owed him a debt. Instead of giving them forgiveness for the debt they owed him he treated them harshly, going so far as to grab them by the throat if they didn't pay the debt. When the master that had forgiven him of his debt heard of how he had abused his debtors he put him in chains until his debt was paid. Jesus finishes that story with this statement: "If you do not forgive men from your heart I will turn you over to the tormentors."

Who are the tormentors? The tormentors are those that you choose not to forgive. You have empowered them to rob you of your peace. Most forgiveness comes from the head and not the heart. We know God tells us if we don't forgive we will not be forgiven. Well that's an arm twister. I don't have any choice. If I'm going to be healed and if I'm going to bring honor to my father I must forgive him of his transgressions from my heart.

I was doing an emotional healing session with a young lady that at the age of eleven years old was tied to a tree for two days and was raped by her brother-in-law. You can only imagine the issues she has dealt with throughout her life. She would later become a Christian.

Honoring her father in his dying stages, she assumed the responsibility of being his caretaker. While tending to her father he makes a pass at her! How despicable! She chose to continue caring for him to his death. How could she do that? She chose by an act of her will, through love and the power of the Holy Spirit, to give him mercy and forgiveness. Only by the love of God can this be done. In honoring our father we are honoring *the* Father.

If you want healing it will begin with forgiveness.

My father and all of his siblings sought their father's love and all of them honored him.
They did so by regularly having a large Sunday afternoon meal with all of the grandchildren included at my grandfather's home. The irony of this is that all

of these children were treated the same by a man that had been so abusive to them. He never once told them that he loved them. Yet they all loved and forgave their dad. It was their choice to be there.

Some of the most glorious days in my life have been when I've been fortunate enough to witness a father fall in the arms of his child and say, "I have not done right. I have done wrong. I am asking you to forgive me. I don't want to ever do this again. If you can find it in your heart, will you forgive me?" When forgiveness is asked for and an apology is offered, not one time have I witnessed a son or daughter say, "I'm not going to forgive you! You're a dirt bag! Burn in hell! I don't care what happens to you!" Not once have I seen that happen. God has instinctively put it in the heart of the child to love their father. If there is brokenness in the father's heart, forgiveness is usually given. Regardless of what the father has done to them a child still reaches out and wants to ask, "Daddy do you love me?" They long to hear the response, "Yes, I love you." That is something that will never ever go away, regardless of how difficult the circumstance may be.

**Share the gospel with your father.**

You might say, "My father is a Christian." Tell him what the Bible says.
You may say, "My daddy's not a Christian." Tell him what the Bible says.
If you had the cure for cancer wouldn't you share it? If you have the cure for sin's debt why can't you share it?

When our family would visit my grandparents I knew what was certain to happen before we said our goodbyes. Dad would go where my grandfather would be reclining on his bed watching television. He would stand in the doorway with tears rolling down his cheeks and plead with his father to accept Christ. The anointing would come on him the same as when he was preaching. He would witness to his dad, "Daddy, Jesus died for you. Jesus loves you. It makes no difference what you've done."

He's speaking to the man that put more pain in his life than any other human being. Yet he's throwing out the lifeline of Jesus. "Daddy, I'm going to have to return to my church. Daddy I can't leave here knowing that you're not right with God!" I heard that for fifteen years of my life until the day he died. My grandfather would sit with a stone face, unmoved by what his son was speaking to him. My father faithfully presented the gospel to his own father.

He would watch Billy Graham and Oral Roberts faithfully on television. He never darkened the church door in my lifetime. I cannot determine his end. That is up to God. We want to believe that he cried out to the Lord in his last waking moments…

It is our responsibility to share the gospel with a father that we cannot respect. By the way, the gospel is *good* news if believed.

**Appreciate the good qualities he exhibits.**

Everyone has some kind of redeeming quality, my grandfather included. When he was an older man I can remember going swimming with him. We would swim in a nearby coal pit. My grandfather could swim with both hands out of the water, both feet out of the water, and whistle amazing grace all at the same time. Now if you think that's easy, let me challenge you to try it. If you're going to float you hold air in your lungs, you don't release it. He could do that. My grandfather was a very wise man when it came to politics and farming crops. Everybody has redeeming qualities.

They may have had some kind of physical attribute like my father, who was exceptionally strong in his prime. They may have a personality trait that brings tremendous humor and laugher to the family. They may be a person that is extremely generous. There is always some redeemable trait in a person. There is something good in everybody that we can focus on. Appreciate the good things about him. Tell your children about the good things.

## Do something for him as an act of kindness.

Send him a gift without it being a special occasion. Call him on the phone and bring him up to date with your life and what's going on. Use a special skill that God has given you. Show up and paint his house or fix a leaky sink unexpectedly. Mow the yard. Do an act of kindness. Not because you feel like it. Not because he's worthy. It's because you are honoring the person that God chose to bring you into the world.

## Choose to speak kindly to him.

Our words are so powerful. James 3:5 says, "The tongue is a small part of the body and yet it boasts of great things. See how great a forest is set afire by such a small fire."

Words can escalate issues quickly. Words can make things much worse than they are presently. Life and death are in the power of the tongue. It has the power to curse or to bless. Choose your words about your father carefully and intentionally. Make a very important choice, and choose to stop placing blame on him.

Have you ever done something so horrible that if everybody knew it you would be embarrassed? I have. How you and I should appreciate the fact that mercy has been given to us! When we show mercy and kindness we are being like Jesus. He told an adulterous woman, "Go and sin no more."

The time will come when you must make a choice to stop blaming. What has happened has happened. You can make a choice to forgive him of all his offenses. You will receive healing for your broken heart by releasing the guilty. You can choose to stop accusing and blaming. It is time to accept responsibility for your own choices about how you deal with offense.

**Write a tribute and give it to him.**

If you don't have anything good to say about him keep it brief. Don't lie to him. The sad reality is it can be very difficult to even present it to him without fear of a negative response. However, we are seeking a way to bring about healing in the relationship. That means that you cannot wait for your father to take the first initiative in attempting to restore the relationship. You, through God, are using the door of honor, to honor God and at the same time create some form of relationship with a father that you have no respect for. By using the method of writing you do not have to be present. He will read it. Once he has read your honest tribute he cannot erase from his mind the words of your heart. It can be a method that can bring healing. Honor is a key to access. It may be the key to restoring the relationship.

**Pray for your father.**

Jesus said in Luke 6:28, "Pray for those who mistreat you." This is one of the most difficult commands that Jesus ever gave to us. Yet, He by example prayed, "Father forgive them for they know not what they do."

What happens when you pray for your father? You are placing him in the hands of God to give him special dealings. The prayer for your father may never change him, but it will change your heart.

As you pray for your father something unusual and miraculous will take place in your heart. You are bringing the one who hurt you and yourself, the one who is hurting, to the Lord.

How long has it been since you and your children prayed for your father? Make it a priority. Make it a daily prayer. I love to hear my grandkids pray. Why? They start out with, "Lord, bless Grams and Gramps, Oma and Papa, Momma and Daddy, etc." They don't stop until they have prayed for every family member. I really like the part where they say, "Lord bless Papa."

Teach your children by praying for your father. It does wonders for the heart. In fact, don't you think that just maybe God might answer your prayer?

As you pray for your father a change will take place in your heart.

**Keep your father connected with your family, as much as wisdom will allow.**

If your father has been a sexual offender or physically abusive, wisdom requires that you do not leave your children alone with him. If it means that your children will be exposed to alcohol don't leave your kids with him. Don't be so religious that you fail to give proper protection that is required of you as a parent.

When relationships are strained it's easy to become withdrawn and distant from each other. When you get in one another's presence there may be awkwardness with how to begin a conversation.

You must determine the level of relationship you want to have with him. One thing is certain, if you make the effort to reconnect with him it may be worth it.

## DISCUSSION QUESTIONS

1. Why should you honor a father you do not respect?

2. What can you do to honor a father you do not respect?

3. If you choose to honor your father will you feel you are excusing his behavior?

4. What is the definition for mercy? Can you give this to your father?

5. How do your children respond to your father's offenses toward you?

6. What are the benefits received from forgiving him?

7. Why should you pray for him?

8. Have you shared the gospel with him?

9. What have you done for your father to honor him?

## Chapter 4

# GIVE ME YOUR PRESENCE

**T**HERE IS NOTHING OUR CHILDREN WANT FROM us more than our presence. A father who spends time with his children places value on his children. I have never met a father who complained about spending too much time with his children, but I have met many who have regretted not spending *enough* time with their children.

I have my own story to share about the presence of a father.

At the age of thirty-nine, I had open-heart surgery. It is quite unusual for a person to have that surgery at such a young age. When they tell you that they are going to open your chest, stop your heart, and put you on a pump for forty-five minutes while they perform surgery, it certainly causes you to face your mortality.

My mother, brother, and close friends were there to pray for me and be with me. An issue with his back would not permit my dad to be present. I was disappointed, of course, but it could not be helped.

At the most crucial time in my life, I did not know that I was about to have one of my greatest encounters with God. God the Father was about to speak to me. When I awakened in the recovery room, immediately I sensed the presence of God. It was as if He were seated in the chair next to my hospital bed.

God spoke to me as clearly as I had ever heard. It was not audible, but it was loud in my spirit. He said, "Your dad could not be with you today, but your Father is here. Glenn, I want you to stop preaching about My power, and preach about My presence. All that the people need is available for them when I am present. Everything is going to be all right."

For the next thirty days, I felt a peace that was unexplainable. I never worried about the church, how my bills would be paid, or even how the family would handle my recovery. That is certainly not normal. The doctors had warned me that depression almost always follows such a serious surgery. It never happened.

I have prayed for that same level of peace to return on several occasions, but it never has. I experienced such peace because my Father was present. Whenever the Father is present, there can be no fear. He said several times through the Bible, "Fear not, for I am with you."

When the Father is present, fear has no choice but to leave. Why?

*1 John 4:18 (KJV):* "There is no fear in love; but perfect love casteth out fear: because fear hath torment. He that feareth is not made perfect in love."

You and I do not have perfect love. But God does. He *is* love! He has perfect love. His presence drives away or casts out fear. It is an open show of force. *Fear must leave.*

The assignment of the devil is to attempt to convince us that God is neither present nor active in our lives.

Like God, your presence has a tremendous effect on your children. When you cannot be with them, the Father is! No wonder David could say in Psalm 23:4, "Even though I walk through the valley of the shadow of death, I will fear no evil, for you are with me."

We can overcome all of life's struggles, uncertainties, and unexpected calamities, as long as we just know that He is with us. The same is true with your family, Dad. Your presence is the key to peace and safety for your family in a time of trouble.

The truth is that God is ever present. Matthew 28:20 says, "And behold, I am with you always, to the end of the age." Whenever a father is present, the environment changes. A child will feel valued and important.

- Children whose fathers are stable and involved are better off on almost every cognitive, social, and emotional measure. For example, high levels of father involvement are correlated with sociability, confidence, and high levels of self-control in children. Moreover, children with involved fathers are less likely to act out in school or engage in risky behaviors in adolescents.
—E. Anther, "Family Guy," *Scientific American Mind*, May/June 2010.

The time you give your children is worth more to them than any *thing* you could ever give them. Memories of doing things together with you will last a lifetime. Not every moment has to be a "Kodak moment." In the *quantity* of time shared with them will come *quality* time. The more time you spend with them, the more they will connect with you. The more you communicate and interact with them, the more they want to be with you. Dad, they really do want to be with you.

How much time do you think the average father spends with his child?

- In two-parent families, children under the age of 13 spent an average of 1.77 hours engaged in activities with their fathers and 2.35 hours doing so with their mothers on a daily basis in 1997. Children in single parent families spent only .42 hours with their fathers and 1.26 hours with their mothers on daily basis.
  —Laura Lippman et al., *Indicators of Child, Family, and Community Connections*. Office of the Assistant Secretary for Planning and Evaluation. Washington, D.C.: US Department of Health and Human Services, 2004.

I played baseball from Little League and all through high school. I was a left-handed pitcher and first baseman. Two professional baseball teams scouted me. My father and mother seldom attended any of my games. Dad knew that I was called to be a minister at a young age, and he did not want me pursuing baseball as a career.

He taught me to keep God first in all things. That meant on nights when we had church, Dad would pull up outside the ballpark and honk the car horn. I knew what it meant—I would be in church come church time, and not at the ballpark.

I only remember Dad coming to two baseball games in my life. But when I saw him and Mom in the stands, I wanted to play better than ever. One of those games was in Baxter Springs, Kansas. My parents and my paternal grandmother were in the stands. I was pumped. That night I pitched a no-hitter and hit a home run.

I believed that when my father was present I could do anything. I was free to be my best. I could excel because he was present. He believed in me. I wanted him to be proud of me.

Like the Heavenly Father, we are to bring joy into our children's lives. It is not the big things that we do or what we provide for them that make them happy. It is the moments when we laugh and do funny things with them that they will remember.

I buried both of my parents within six months of each other. A few days after they passed, my brother and I walked into the house our parents had lived in for over thirty years. I felt nothing. It was just an empty house. What had made that house so special—the place we called home—was the presence of those who lived in it.

Like that empty house, our families, church, and individual lives are empty without His presence. However, when we are in His presence, there is no other place we would rather be.

When you come home, do your children run to you, excited to see you, or do they continue whatever they are doing, without response? If they do not acknowledge your presence, it may be that you need to bring some joy into the house!

*Psalm 16:11:* "In your presence there is fullness of joy."

*2 Corinthians 3:17:* "Now the Lord is the Spirit, and where the Spirit of the Lord is, there is freedom."

My father saw to it that our home was a fun place. The best part of the day was when we were at the dinner table. Dad would tell funny stories, and sometimes spontaneous things would happen that would cause us to break out in laughter.

Evangelist Dennis Thrasher was having dinner in our home on a nice summer day. We had eaten a wonderful home-cooked meal and were enjoying the conversation when Dad excused himself from the table. He said he must finish mowing the yard before dark.

The rest of us remained at the table and continued our conversation. The window had been raised near the dining table because the temperature outside was so nice. Dad stuck out his tongue at all of us as he passed by the window on his riding lawn mower.

Dennis said, "I ought to throw a glass of cold water on him the next time he passes."

My mother immediately responded by saying, "Go ahead. I dare you."

The next time Dad passed by the window, Dennis threw cold water on him through the window screen. Dad kept mowing like nothing had happened. But the next time he passed the window, he had a garden hose in his hand, and he sprayed water inside the house on everyone sitting at the table. That was my dad!

You can teach your family how to celebrate the goodness of God and what He has done for your family. Your home should be so much like heaven that if an angel were to visit it, he would think he was still in heaven.

Thanksgiving and Christmas were times of the year that Dad and Mom wanted the entire family to be together. The house would be filled with sounds of laughter, singing, jokes, stories, and ball games. Before each meal, Dad would tearfully offer thanks to God for His goodness on our family, and bless the food. When dinner was finished, Dad would retire to his easy chair.

There, he would shut out the noise that everyone was making and go into the presence of the Lord. He would, on most occasions, break out in prayer and thanksgiving to the Lord for His blessings on our family.

It was not uncommon for Dad to start praying in tongues or praying in English at any time or any place. The last time we all were together, I said to my brother, "Do you realize how blessed and fortunate we are to have such a man as our dad? Just think about the families that never witnessed the joy of an experience like this."

Dad practiced the presence of God. Now Dad's presence is gone. The house is silent. However, the Father remains with us, and we continue to have reasons for joy and celebration.

A church is like a family. If it is devoid of the Father's presence, it is no different than the schoolhouse.

When we are in the presence of our Father, shouldn't it be a time of freedom and joy? What is it like in heaven, where the Father dwells? There is rejoicing in heaven over one sinner who repents. The angels never stop worshipping and crying, "Holy, Holy, Holy," day or night. They sing the song of Moses and the Lamb. Heaven is filled with joy and merrymaking.

The entire house of Israel would break into celebration when the ark returned. It meant that the presence of the Lord was returning to Israel.

*2 Samuel 6:5:* "And David and all the house of Israel were celebrating before the LORD, with songs and lyres and harps and tambourines and castanets and cymbals."

No wonder David danced before the Lord. He had missed the presence of God. The presence of the Lord was back in Israel, as indicated by the presence of the ark. It was a time for music and merrymaking.

What is heaven celebrating? The Father's presence! What were David and Israel celebrating? The Father's presence! What should your family be celebrating? The Father's presence!

In the same way, your family should celebrate because you, the father, are with them. Being with them makes room for precious opportunities for them to share what is happening in their lives: their issues, stresses, fears, dreams, and more. Your concentrated, concerned, and listening ear is so important. They will feel more valued because you took the time to listen.

When a father is present with his family, all those who are in the home should feel safe and at rest. That indeed is how the presence of God our Father affects us.

*Exodus 33:14:* "And he said, 'My presence will go with you, and I will give you rest.'"

Dad, will you give them more of your presence?

## DISCUSSION QUESTIONS

1. What steps have you taken to ensure that each of your children has a special time with you that is not shared with others?

2. Does the environment of the home change when you come in from work?

3. What must leave when the Father is present? Why?

4. Does your example support God being first in the home?

5. Share a humorous story of something that happened while you were at home with the children.

6. Do your children celebrate you? Do you celebrate them?

Chapter 5

# I WANT TO BE "SO LOVED"

**A** FATHER WHO LIVES ON A GOLF COURSE where I am a member has impressed me because of the special care he provides for his special needs son. His adult son is severely handicapped, both mentally and physically. The son is unable to communicate with anyone.

This father has taken on a responsibility that not many would. His wife was sick with cancer for several years. The added burden of caring for his wife while continuing to care for his son would have overwhelmed the average man. He is not a young father. This dad is in his early seventies. Now, after the loss of his wife, he continues to provide the best of care for his son.

During the warm months of the year, it is not uncommon to see this dad and his son on their golf cart going around the course. They stop and talk to the golfers, and he points out certain beauties of the course to his son. He converses with him as though he understands every word. He tells him he loves him and what he means to him.

At an opportune time, I shared with him that he was one of the most devoted fathers I had ever observed. This observation took him by surprise. His expression seemed to say, "What am I doing that every other father would not do?" It seemed as though what he did was not a burden at all, but rather a privilege.

In reality, this does not happen often. His response to me was, "I love him so much!"

His words, without doubt, capture the heart of God found in John 3:16: "For God so loved the world."

Do you know what it is like to be "so loved"? Through the years dealing with people in emotional healing, I have learned there are many in the church who struggle with understanding the Father's love. Their fathers were either absent in their lives or were abusive to them.

A young college student recently attended our Wednesday night prayer meeting for the second time and was deeply moved. I was visiting with her after service and expressing our appreciation for her attendance, when she broke down in tears. She said, "When I went up front as the church people were praying for needs, I felt something come over me. I was afraid."

I quickly responded, "I know what that is. It is the love of God the Father." Discerning that this was a divine appointment, I continued to press her about her relationship with God. She stated that she knew that God loved her, but she was afraid of Him.

I said, "Tell me, how has your father treated you? What kind of a relationship have you had with your father?"

She could not hold back the emotions of a past traumatic experience. She blurted out in a painful and distraught voice, "My natural father molested me when I was a child!"

I said to her, "That explains it. Because we call God 'Father,' you relate to Him in the same manner you do your natural father. But God is a perfect Father. He does not love unnaturally. His love is pure and kind. You are safe in His love."

After praying that the Lord would remove her fear of Him, I prayed that the shame and the words that were spoken over her by her father would be broken off of her. I prayed she would claim her innocence in Jesus and know that she was worthy to be loved and was free to love God the Father in return. An immediate peace came over her. The fear was gone. She expressed her peace with a warm smile and thankfulness to the Lord instead of tears.

A person who has not experienced a father's love will most often struggle with receiving the Father's love.

In an emotional healing setting, I was ministering to a young man who could not understand what love was. This was his story: His father was an alcoholic. Almost every night of his childhood, his father got drunk, came into his bedroom while he was asleep, and urinated on him. While he was doing this, he told his son how worthless and no good he was.

Is it any wonder that this young man would struggle with a father's love?

In my recent book *Out of the Snare*, I shared the following observation. I asked a counselor friend, "Why, when my father reads the Bible, does he always see judgment? He preaches a lot on judgment. When I read the Bible I see love, forgiveness, mercy, blessing, etc. I preach a lot on the favor and love of God. Why are we so different when we have the same Bible?"

He responded with a question: "What kind of father did your dad have, and what was your relationship like with your father?"

I said, "Dad had a physically and emotionally abusive father. My dad, on the other hand, was a wonderful father who loved me and was good to me."

He said, "There is your answer. You perceive God by the relationship you have had with your earthly father."

My father recently died at the age of ninety-one. His father never told him he loved him. My father made a decision that his sons would never be deprived of hearing the most important words in the world: "I love you." I heard those words many times throughout my life. Whenever I returned home to visit, Dad met me at the door with his frail arms outstretched, saying, "Oh son, I love you so much! I have missed you so badly. Son, I wish you didn't live so far away. I love you, son."

Though he was old and feeble, his words were always affirming, placing value and importance on me. Those words have carried me in my most difficult times. I will never forget them. How I wish I could hear them now. What an example he was to me of how a father's love is expressed.

This is something I do not want to lose. I have raised my family to be huggers and to speak "I love you" to one another. It makes no difference where we meet. In public or at home, we openly express our love for each other.

God the Father is the perfect example for us to emulate. He demonstrates how we are to "so love."

## So Loved—Verbally

Our children deserve and desire our words of love. They must *hear* our words of love. Our Heavenly Father demonstrated this for us at the Jordan River. As Jesus came out of the water, after being baptized by John the Baptist, what happened? God spoke audibly. What did He say?

*Matthew 3:17:* "This is my beloved Son, with whom I am well pleased."

# I WANT TO BE "SO LOVED"

The words you speak—whether spoken in love or without love—will shape your child's future, either positively or negatively.

Iva was an elderly lady who made life difficult for many people. She would stand at the front door of the church and deliberately make statements that would offend people as they were entering.

From day one of my becoming the pastor of the church, she made life difficult for me. I did not understand why she acted the way she did. Because of her offensive words, people called her "Poison Ivy" behind her back.

Out of exasperation, I prayed and asked God how I should deal with this woman. The Lord gave me a very direct instruction: "Love her." My response was, "How can I love her when she attacks me with the intent of making me upset? Lord, You will have to teach me how to love her!" That is exactly what He did.

I began to look for positive ways to compliment her truthfully. As soon as she entered the church, I'd hug her and brag about her being one of the best-dressed ladies in the church. Before she could open her mouth to say anything, I'd hug her and tell her I loved her. It caught her off guard. She didn't know how to respond. It completely disarmed her.

The Lord had given me a very important key to help Iva. He pointed out to me that Iva had been married for several years and had no children. She loved children. She taught a children's Sunday school class. Almost every Sunday, she would ask if she could take my three-year-old daughter Lisa for ice cream. Lisa loved going with her.

Over time, Iva began to change for the better. She lost her aggressiveness and stopped attacking people with her words. She lost much of her hostility. She became much more approachable.

I will never forget the day that Iva came to my home, weeping to the point that her words were difficult to understand. Immediately I thought someone had died in her family or that some tragedy had occurred.

"Iva, what is wrong?" I asked.

She responded, "I just left the nursing home where my father is dying. He is well into his nineties, and today, for the first time in my life, he told me he loved me!"

Suddenly, what the Holy Spirit had told me to do was validated. Now I knew why she was so unpleasant and acting out. It was to get attention, even if it was for negative reasons. Her life had been miserable because she had never heard those important words from her father. The need of her life was to be "so loved."

A very personable, attractive, and gifted young lady disclosed to me that her father had never told her she was pretty or that he loved her. Some time later I asked the father without reference to his daughter why he could not tell his children he loved them.

"I just can't," he responded.

Without backing away, I said, "It's your body. You can do what you want with it."

Exasperated, he replied, "No I can't."

"Why?"

"Because I was never told I was loved," he said.

A short time passed, and his daughter came up to me in service, grinning and weeping at the same time. She said, "You will never believe what my daddy told me this week. He told me that I was beautiful, that he loved me, and that he was proud of me."

Just those few words changed the way she felt about herself. The struggle for affirmation was gone. Those words freed his daughter to feel worthy of being loved.

Every son or daughter deserves to hear these words from their father:

- Nothing or no one is more important to me than you.
- You are Daddy's best friend.
- I am so proud of you.
- You can accomplish anything in life you want to accomplish.
- I believe in you.
- I will always love you.

Your children will become the people you tell them they are. If you bless them, they will accomplish more than you ever expected them to. They will become the people whose self-portrait you have framed with your words.

## So Loved—with Affection and Touch

Josh McDowell tells about entering a gym during a basketball game, looking for his son. He walked down the sidelines, looking up into the bleachers for him. His son stood up, unnoticed by him, and came down the steps at midcourt to meet his dad. Without thinking, they embraced in front of the entire audience. It was their custom every time they met to hug. They thought nothing of it.

To their amazement, a chant began to rise from the crowd: "I wish you were my dad. I wish you were my dad."

Today's generation is longing to be loved by their fathers, openly and unashamedly. The young men who are in your circle of relationships and influence, I assure you, are longing for a father figure. They are seeking a man who will love them and mentor them to be their best.

Why are hugs and kisses so important? We are told that children who do not receive touching and holding in their infancy can die or be underdeveloped in their learning. Researchers conducted a study examining father involvement in the lives of 134 children of adolescent mothers. They concluded that during the first ten years of life the father-child contact was associated with better socio-emotional and academic functioning.

- Researchers conducted a study examining father involvement in the lives of 134 children of adolescent mothers. They concluded that during the first ten years of life, the father-child contact was associated with better socio-emotional and academic functioning. These results indicated that children with more involved fathers experienced fewer behavioral problems and scored higher on reading achievement. This study showed the significance of the role of fathers in the lives of at-risk children, even in case of non-resident fathers.
  —K.S. Howard, Burke Lefever, J.E., J.G. Borkowski, and T.L. Whitman, "Fathers' Influence in the Lives of Children with Adolescent Mothers" *Journal of Family Psychology 2006*. Vol. 20, No. 3, 468–476

- Premature infants who have increased visits from their fathers during hospitalization have improved weight gain and score higher on developmental tests.
  —W.L. Coleman, C.F. Garfield, and the Committee on Psychosocial Aspects of Child and Family Health, "Fathers and Pediatricians: Enhancing Men's Roles in the Care and Development of their Children—American Academy of Pediatrics Policy Statement," *Pediatrics*, May 2004.

A man was raised in a home where his father never touched him or spoke to him. His mother cared for him, but his father treated him like he did not exist. Literally, it was like he was never in the room.

## I WANT TO BE "SO LOVED"

Needless to say, he struggled with his identity, his self-worth, and knowing a father's love. It caused him to act out in a very dysfunctional way that I will not share with you. However, in the emotional healing room, he shared that his father had only touched him once in his life. It was when his father kneed him in the groin. Because of this action, and his desperate need for his father's affection and attention, he associated love with pain.

This interpretation of pain being associated with love is one that I have heard several times throughout the years. Pure, heartfelt affection will ensure that our children will know the value of love being given and received in a healthy manner.

Your hugs and kisses will make your children the affectionate spouse their future spouse will need them to be.

A common problem in many marriages is lack of affection from a spouse. In most cases, it is because the spouse was never the recipient of pure affection. It is not uncommon that they may have experienced a sexual trauma at some point in life. They are uncomfortable with giving something that they have not experienced: honest and pure affection. It feels strange and awkward to them. Holding hands, kissing, or touching is an awkward experience for them to give or receive.

If you want your children to have to have healthy marriages, then give them lots of affection and touching.

> *"Words of love without touch are like a wrapped gift with nothing in it."*
>
> —*Shirel Renneker*

## So Loved—Impartially

What happens when one child is favored above another? This becomes the seedbed for jealousy, insecurity, and rejection.

Isaac and Rebekah had a dysfunctional home. They each had a favored son. Isaac loved Esau because he was a man of the field. Rebekah loved Jacob because he was a man of the house. This issue of favoritism would continue into the next generation. Jacob, like his father, became a father of favorites.

*Genesis 37:3:* "Israel loved Joseph more than any other of his sons."

He loved Joseph more than his other sons because of his love for Rachel, the wife whom he loved. The sons of Leah were never recipients of the love that was lavishly given to Joseph. When Jacob gave Joseph that famous coat of many colors, it created a jealousy in the brothers so great that they desired to murder him. They could not even speak well of him.

Children of blended families often have issues concerning favoritism, as this data reflects.

- A sample of 4,027 resident fathers and children from the Fragile Families and Child Well-Being Survey was used to investigate the effects of a biological father's multi-partner fertility on adolescent health. The study indicated that fathers' depression and lack of involvement in the children's lives help to account for child behavior problems and deficient physical health.—J. Bronte-Tinkew, A. Horowitz, and M.E. Scott, "Fathering with Multiple Partners: Links to Children's Well-Being in Early Childhood, *Journal of Marriage and Family*, 71, pp. 608–631, 2009.

# I WANT TO BE "SO LOVED"

Too often in emotional healing sessions, I have been told the following:
- My father showed affection to my brothers and sisters, but never to me.
- My father loved the dogs more than he loved me.
- My father affirmed my siblings, but spoke curses over me because I looked liked my mother. He didn't like her.
- My father did not love me like the others because my interest was not in sports or hunting. Because I liked music, art, and creativity, he would have nothing to do with me. He called me a sissy.

We can learn how to be better fathers by observing how our Heavenly Father expresses His love for us. How does He love? He shows no favoritism.

*Acts 10:34 (NLT):* "Then Peter replied, 'I see very clearly that God shows no favoritism.'"

*Romans 2:11 (NLT):* "For God does not show favoritism."

Receive this truth for yourself. Practice this truth before your children.

My father was meticulous about how he treated his children and grandchildren. He kept records of how much money he spent on each of us. What one received, we all received. Can you imagine how this made us feel? The message was loud and clear: "I love you all the same!"

"For God so loved the world" means *everyone*. How does God convince us that He loves us? The following Scriptures demonstrate the love that God has shown us by sending His Son to the cross to bring us all into His favor.

*1 John 4:9 (NLT):* "God showed how much he loved us by sending his one and only Son into the world so that we might have eternal life through him."

*Romans 5:8 (NLT):* "But God showed his great love for us by sending Christ to die for us while we were still sinners."

*John 15:13:* "Greater love has no one than this, that someone lay down his life for his friends."

What the Father has proven is that He loves us all equally. He has demonstrated it by giving the life of His Son. There is no greater love than this! The Father wants us to know that He loves us all. He has no favorites!

## So Loved—Unconditionally

When we make purposeful efforts to demonstrate our love for our children, they will love us in return as their father. God the Father, again, is our role model.

*1 John 4:19 (KJV):* "We love him, because he first loved us."

Do you remember when you first saw your baby? It was love at first sight. Why? Because it was yours! You created that baby through the bond of love. There was nothing this child had to do to earn your love; you gave it freely, without condition. Before the child was mature enough to understand your sacrifice, provision, and unconditional love, you were there, always giving your expressions of love.

As a teenager, because I did not particularly care about being around children, I had the absurd idea that I would not be able to love my own children. Then, when my baby girl was born, the doctor introduced her to me in the hallway of the hospital. I said, "Look, what long fingers. What big feet!"

The doctor interrupted me with, "Hey, son, this is *your* daughter, not someone else's, that you're talking about!"

It hit me like a ton of bricks. I was overwhelmed by the very thought of being a father. Immediately the concerns for the future care of this baby placed fear in

## I WANT TO BE "SO LOVED"

me. My mind was immediately filled with questions—Could I take care of her when she was sick? Would I be able to provide for all of her personal needs?

When I saw her the second time, my father was present with me. I asked him, "Dad, what do you think she will become?" He responded with an answer that would put me on course as a father for the rest of my life:

"Son, she will be whatever you teach her to be."

The word *father* means "creator." Our Father is the one responsible for bringing us into the world. He gave us life and, with that life, a purpose for being. It is His will for us to discover it and live it out, by His grace and guidance.

Like God, as a father you are responsible for molding your children into the people God has purposed for them to become.

Have you ever been asked any of these questions?

- Why did you father me?
- Did you want me?
- Am I the gender you wanted me to be?
- If I am not like the others, will you still love me?
- If I fail, will you still love me?
- If I mess up or embarrass you, will you still love me?

If you have been asked these questions, it is evidence that you have failed in conveying the message of your love as a father. If you have asked these questions yourself, it's a clear indication that you feel you are not good enough and must do more to be loved.

All of these questions stem from wanting unconditional love. If you are loved unconditionally, there is no need to compare yourself to your siblings. You will never be like them. You can only be who God has created you to be.

Comparison is a clear indication of conditional love. Comparison with others can be a motive for not improving yourself.

As fathers, we play a major part in making our children who they will be spiritually, emotionally, and physically. What we see in our children is a reflection of ourselves.

One of the saddest young ladies I ever met was a daughter of a very successful businessman. He had five children early in his marriage. Because of the financial stress of being a provider, he worked long and hard hours.

In time, he became the owner of two businesses that required even more of his time. His children were now approaching college age. His daughter, whom I will call Rachel, desperately needed her father's unconditional love.

Rachel was different from her siblings. She did not have the appearance of an average young lady. She worked at male-type jobs. She dressed more like a male than a female. She was a hard worker.

One day she came in weeping and knelt in front of her father, who was sitting in his chair in the family room. She said through her tears, "All my life I have tried to please you. I have done things I didn't want to do, just to get your attention. You acted like you didn't want me to be a daughter, so I worked like a man, dressed like a man—and none of what I have done is good enough. I can't take it anymore. Do you love me? What do I have to do to get your favor or attention? Would you please tell me that I am a pretty girl?"

A father has the power to release his children to become everything God created them to become. Our Heavenly Father has done just that! He has released us to become all that we were created to be.

He has released us to believe that we can and will succeed.

*Philippians 4:13 (KJV):* "I can do all things through Christ which strengtheneth me."

## I WANT TO BE "SO LOVED"

*Matthew 17:20:* "Jesus said to them, 'Because of your little faith. For truly, I say to you, if you have faith like a grain of mustard seed, you will say to this mountain, "Move from here to there," and it will move, and nothing will be impossible for you.'"

As a father, what is the greatest gift you can give your child?

> *"My father gave me the greatest gift anyone could give another person: he believed in me."*
> —*Jim Valvano*

The Bible tells us that the Heavenly Father has adopted us.

*Romans 8:15 (KJV):* "For ye have not received the spirit of bondage again to fear; but ye have received the Spirit of adoption, whereby we cry, Abba, Father."

Adoption is when the parents choose the child, not when the child chooses the parents.

*Ephesians 1:4–5 (KJV):* "According as he hath chosen us in him before the foundation of the world, that we should be holy and without blame before him in love: having predestinated us unto the adoption of children by Jesus Christ to himself, according to the good pleasure of his will."

He has chosen us in Christ. How does that make you feel? You are special!

Our children want to be like us. My brother Darrell has taken on the look and actions of my father. I always wanted people to tell me that I favored my dad as well, but it seldom happened. I loved him so much; I wanted to be like him.

# FATHER ME

My wife told me recently, "You didn't get any of your looks from your father. If anything, you got them from your mother. You even walk like your mother!" That will do something for your male ego.

When God the Father created man, He created us in His image and likeness. We are like Him. He sees himself in us. Because we are in Christ, the Heavenly Father sees us as righteous and blameless. He sees us as a reflection of himself.

*Romans 8:29:* "For those whom he foreknew he also predestined to be conformed to the image of his Son."

*2 Corinthians 5:21:* "For our sake he made him to be sin who knew no sin, so that in him we might become the righteousness of God."

When God looks at us, He sees a reflection of His own righteousness! He has made us like His Son.

Our children must know that our love is bestowed upon them without conditions. The Heavenly Father again is our example of how we are to love. He bestows His love on us!

*1 John 3:1 (KJV):* "Behold [stop and consider], what manner of love the Father hath bestowed [given as a gift] upon us, that we should be called the sons of God."

To be "so loved" is to be loved beyond measure.

*Ephesians 3:17–19 (NLT):* "Then Christ will make his home in your hearts as you trust in him. Your roots will grow down into God's love and keep you strong. And may you have the power to understand, as all God's people should, how wide, how long, how high, and how deep his love is. May you experience the love of Christ, though it is too great to understand fully. Then you will be made complete with all the fullness of life and power that comes from God."

# I WANT TO BE "SO LOVED"

A bestowed love is one that is given without expectations. It is a love that doesn't have to be earned. I want to know that you love me regardless of how much I please or disappoint you. If I rob a bank, will you still love me? If I steal something, will you still love me? If I do not go to college, will you still love me?

"Bestowed love" is that spoken of by Paul in 1 Corinthians.

*1 Corinthians 13:4,6–7 (NLT):* "Love is patient and kind...[it] rejoices whenever the truth wins out. Love never gives up, never loses faith, is always hopeful, and endures through every circumstance."

The parable that Jesus told about the prodigal son reveals the unconditional love a father is to have toward his son. The parable is not focused on a wayward son but on the love of a father that is demonstrated to both of his sons.

Can you imagine the embarrassment of the prodigal as he returned to his father, having squandered his inheritance? Can you imagine the shame and embarrassment he felt by discrediting the family name? He must have felt self-conscious for returning with the smell of swine on his clothes. I am certain he did not know what his father's response would be.

Do you remember the expressions of love the father gave to his prodigal son when he returned home?

*Luke 15:20–23 (NLT):* "So he returned home to his father. And while he was still a long way off, his father saw him coming. Filled with love and compassion, he ran to his son, embraced him, and kissed him. His son said to him, 'Father, I have sinned against both heaven and you, and I am no longer worthy of being called your son.' But his father said to the servants, 'Quick! Bring the finest robe in the house and put it on him. Get a ring for his finger and sandals for his feet. And kill the calf we have been fattening. We must celebrate with a feast.'"

That is what unconditional love is like from a godly father. Because his son had found himself, the father affirmed him by giving him fully restored family status. The best robe, a ring, shoes for his feet, and a celebration of his return with a steak dinner said it all! "You are my son, and I love you! Welcome home."

If you will "so love" your children, they will not disappoint you. They will become self-confident and successful in life. Why? You have affirmed them with words, loved them with affectionate touch, loved them with impartiality, and loved them unconditionally. You have given them a true reflection of God the Father.

The Father does not allow anything or anyone to interfere with His love for His children.

*Romans 8:35,38–39 (KJV)*: "Who shall separate us from the love of Christ? Shall tribulation, or distress, or persecution, or famine, or nakedness, or peril, or sword?...For I am persuaded, that neither death, nor life, nor angels, nor principalities, nor powers, nor things present, nor things to come, nor height, nor depth, nor any other creature, shall be able to separate us from the love of God, which is in Christ Jesus our Lord."

Father, we receive Your love now. Thank You, Father, for "so loving"!

Dad, will you "so love" your children?

## DISCUSSION QUESTIONS

1. Why might a person struggle with understanding the love of God?

2. How would you define your relationship with your father? What impact has it had in your life?

3. Do you often verbally express your love to your children? What do you say to them?

4. Did your father verbally express his love for you?

5. List some of the many benefits that one receives from a father's hugs and touch.

6. How does a person respond to God the Father if his siblings are given more attention than he receives?

7. How would your children describe your love for them?

8. Explain what unconditional love is.

## Chapter 6

# PROTECT ME

**A** YOUNG PERSON WHO HAS WITNESSED THE ABUSE of a parent, heard his or her parents arguing loudly late into the night, or has been raped, molested, or physically abused will have deep issues with fear that will carry over into adult life. Because a father was not there to protect them, they feel extremely vulnerable to violence. Regardless of why the father was not present, the impact of not being rescued or defended remains the same.

When children come forward with what has happened and are not defended or believed, their fear issues will grow greater. The false guilt and fears they feel about themselves are compounded. They may accept blame for what has happened to them. Often they withdraw into a shell of privacy and secrecy about their personal struggle with the event. They no longer talk about it.

Our children must have our protection and be defended by us when it is necessary!

As a father, I have raised my children to believe that the safest place in the entire world is in their father's arms. There is nothing and no one whom I would knowingly allow to harm one of my children. I will protect my children at all costs. I will deplete every resource I have before my children will fall prey to danger.

*Psalm 63:8:* "My soul clings to you; your right hand upholds me."

In life's most threatening moments, we must remind ourselves that when we are in danger, our Father's hand will deliver us.

I will never forget an event from my childhood that reminds me of how my father's hand could save me. My dad took me fishing at a river near where we lived. We fished for a while and caught nothing.

Dad was never satisfied with where we fished. We could always catch them on the other side of the river, he was sure. On this particular day, he grabbed all the fishing equipment with one hand and held onto my hand with the other. We waded into a shallow riffle in the river. What was about waist-high on my dad was up to my neck. I was exceedingly fearful that I would be swept away by the swiftness of the current that increased as we continued to cross the river.

The river current was not only swift, but the rocks underwater were covered with a slick moss that made it even more difficult to stand or hold your position. Suddenly my feet slipped out from under me, and my body was lifted to the top of the river. I felt the force of the current attempting to rip me out of my father's grasp.

I began to cry and scream, knowing that this would be my death. Calmly, my father increased his grip on my hand. He said, "Son, Daddy will keep you safe. I am larger and taller than you. Daddy will see to it that you make it safely to the other side." Within a few seconds, my feet felt the rocks again, and we were in much calmer water. My father had kept his word.

## PROTECT ME

Our Father's grip is stronger than ours. We feel that we must hold His hand, when in reality He is holding ours. The safest place in the world is remaining in our Father's hand. He has a grip on our life and will not turn us loose.

*John 10:28–29:* "I give them eternal life, and they will never perish, and no one will snatch them out of my hand. My Father, who has given them to me, is greater than all, and no one is able to snatch them out of the Father's hand."

Two times in these verses, Jesus makes it clear to us to why we are safe. No one can snatch us out of our Father's hand!

As a small boy, I would match my hand with Dad's for comparison. His hands seemed to be as large as the world, compared to mine. Have you ever thought about the size of our Father's hands?

*Isaiah 40:12:* "Who has measured the waters in the hollow of his hand and marked off the heavens with a span, enclosed the dust of the earth in a measure and weighed the mountains in scales and the hills in a balance?"

Amazing! Our Father measured the waters in the palm of *one hand*, and measured the heavens with His hands. Those hands have the power to keep us safe from all harm.

What happens when the enemy of our soul attempts to rip us out of our Father's hand? Our Father will fight for us!

*Deuteronomy 3:22:* "It is the Lord your God who fights for you."

*Deuteronomy 20:4 (NKJV):* "For the Lord your God is He who goes with you, to fight for you against your enemies, to save you."

As a child, I believed there was not a man on earth who was stronger than my father. We must be reminded of who is protecting us—God the Father!

# FATHER ME

The Bible speaks explicitly about the power of our Father's right hand.

*Exodus 15:6:* "Your right hand, O Lord, glorious in power, your right hand, O Lord, shatters the enemy."

*Psalm 138:7:* "Though I walk in the midst of trouble, you preserve my life; you stretch out your hand against the wrath of my enemies, and your right hand delivers me."

How many times have you been in a circumstance where it appeared there was no way out? You came so close to dying in an accident, yet you escaped without explanation. You overdosed and lived. You almost gave up in deep water, but suddenly your feet touched bottom. You were ready to pull the trigger and end it all, but someone walked in and stopped you.

Do you think it was coincidence or mere chance that you survived?

Stanley Renneker was following a large truck on a highway. He could not see around it to determine whether it was safe to pass. In a split second, he decided to pass the truck. As he attempted to change lanes, a voice spoke loudly to him, "No!" He quickly switched back into his own lane of traffic. In an instant, the tailwind from another large truck caused his car to sway as it roared past him. If he had not listened, he and his wife would be dead today. Thank God for His mighty right hand.

As a teenager, I worked the wheat harvest from Texas to the Canadian border. I drove a combine in the fields and a truck to deliver the grain to the storage bins.

We had worked late one evening after dark. I still had to deliver the grain before the dew settled. My truck was loaded, and I was on my way to the bins. I was on a deserted Nebraska country road in the middle of nowhere with no traffic around. When a grain truck is full, it is difficult to stop it quickly, because when the brake is applied, the grain shifts, causing the weight to transfer to the front of the truck.

My mind was not on where I was as I approached the main highway. I looked to the right and saw a vehicle approaching at a high rate of speed. I knew I was going too fast to stop in time, but I repeatedly hit the brake in a panicked attempt to slow the truck down.

With my eyes closed, I cried out to God for help. I knew without a doubt I was going to enter the highway in the path of that oncoming vehicle. Suddenly, without explanation, it was as though two hands were restraining my truck. I watched as the vehicle passed in front of me in a flash. I had come to a stop on the yellow line in the center of the highway. Thank God for His saving power!

One of the struggles we face in life is the feeling of *vulnerability*. It is a feeling of having no walls of protection. It is a feeling of being defenseless. You are not defenseless! Your Father is defending you. He will not allow anything to take your life until you have fulfilled your life's purpose.

Consider the three Hebrews, Shadrach, Meshach, and Abed-nego. They had no power to defend or protect themselves from the edict of the king. He declared they were to bow and worship a false god. They refused, knowing the sentence would be a fiery furnace. When they were cast into the furnace, they were not burned. There was a fourth man in the fire, who had the appearance of the Son of God, who saved their lives. They came out without a hair on their heads being singed, their clothes unharmed, and not even the smell of smoke on them!

Their leader Daniel was discovered praying, also in violation of the king's decree. He, too, would suffer the consequences. He was thrown into a den of hungry lions, but was miraculously saved because the Lord closed the mouths of the lions.

I call that protection. Are you any less important to your Father than these people? He has promised us His protection.

*Isaiah 54:17:* "No weapon that is fashioned against you shall succeed, and you shall refute every tongue that rises against you in judgment."

The Lord will not only protect you from life-threatening situations, but He will also defend you from those who attack your reputation and character. There is no weapon that destroys or wounds more quickly than the human tongue.

*Psalm 31:19–20:* "Oh, how abundant is your goodness, which you have stored up for those who fear you and worked for those who take refuge in you, in the sight of the children of mankind! In the cover of your presence you hide them from the plots of men; you store them in your shelter from the strife of tongues."

Your Father has protected you from many plots that have been set against you that you had no knowledge of. Words have been spoken about you and against you that you have never been permitted to hear.

Why were you unaware of them? His presence became your shelter. He would not allow you to be wounded at that specific time, because you could not deal with it. His presence protected you from having a broken spirit.

Jacob is a good example of how God protects us from threats and harmful words. Jacob left Laban, his father-in-law, because he was a threat to him. He was fearful of bodily harm.

*Genesis 31:7:* "Yet your father has cheated me and changed my wages ten times. But God did not permit him to harm me."

## PROTECT ME

*Genesis 31:29:* "It is in my power to do you harm. But the God of your father spoke to me last night, saying, 'Be careful not to say anything to Jacob, either good or bad.'"

It is God who restrained Laban from speaking threatening words that would have wounded the heart of Jacob and his family. Your Father has covered you with His presence and closed the mouths of those who would oppose your life's purpose many times.

Throughout the life of Christ, the enemies of Jesus plotted, schemed, and did all in their power to make Him appear to be a devil and a drunkard. They even attempted to throw Him off a cliff. But they could not be successful because it was neither the time nor the way Jesus was to give His life.

Various attempts were also made on the life of the apostle Paul. A certain group of men took an oath that they would not eat until Paul was dead. Surviving a shipwreck from a storm, Paul made it to shore only to have a deadly serpent bite him. The people waited, watching to see if he would die. He did not. Why? It was not his time to die. It had been prophesied that he would go to Rome as a witness, and go he did.

Upon his arrival there, he wrote 2 Timothy 4:6–7, "For I am already being poured out as a drink offering, and the time of my departure has come. I have fought the good fight, I have finished the race, I have kept the faith."

No one could take Paul's life until it was his time!

My father was called to pastor a church that was quite legalistic. It was a divided body of believers. The fruit that church produced was far from love. There were vicious attacks on the message of repentance that my father continued to preach for a season, as well as criticism of his leadership.

The Holy Spirit would reveal the issues that were in the church in a supernatural way. Dad could not sleep one night, so he prayed silently most of the night. He asked the Lord to inform him of what was causing him to lose his peace. He also asked for wisdom to handle whatever came to light.

The next morning at breakfast, Dad asked Mom if she knew she had spoken in tongues in her sleep. She laughed and said, "Buford, you're kidding me. No, I didn't know. Why?"

Dad responded, "Last night I could not sleep, and I was praying. I asked God for insight and wisdom about the church. You slowly raised your hands and spoke in other tongues. You went from that to interpreting what you had spoken into English. You told me what was happening and how to handle it. God used you to answer my prayer."

Needless to say, my mother was overwhelmed. Dad followed the instructions of the Holy Spirit, and the church grew and experienced revival. My father was protected, and so was the church body.

Your Father *is* protecting you! He has placed angels around you on assignment for your protection.

*Psalm 34:7:* "The angel of the Lord encamps around those who fear him, and delivers them."

He sent the captain of the Lord's army before Israel to guarantee their victory. When an army surrounded Elisha and his servant Gehazi, Elisha prayed that his servant could see what he was seeing. Immediately the spiritual eyes of Gehazi were opened, and he saw an army of horses and fiery chariots surrounding them both. They had protection. *We* have protection!

His arms are underneath you. They will not allow you to fall.

# PROTECT ME

*Deuteronomy 33:27:* "The eternal God is your dwelling place, and underneath are the everlasting arms."

The Father hovers over you.

*Psalm 91:4 (NLT):* "He will cover you with his feathers. He will shelter you with his wings. His faithful promises are your armor and protection."

Covering us with His feathers is a picture of the Father protecting us from danger. It is the same picture that Jesus gives us in Matthew 23:37, "How often would I have gathered your children together as a hen gathers her brood under her wings, and you were not willing!"

The Holy Spirit is in you.

*Romans 8:11 (NLT):* "The Spirit of God, who raised Jesus from the dead, lives in you. And just as God raised Christ Jesus from the dead, he will give life to your mortal bodies by this same Spirit living within you."

*1 John 4:4:* "Little children, you are from God and have overcome them, for he who is in you is greater than he who is in the world."

He has given us His armor. More specifically, He has given *you* His armor to protect you from the attacks of the enemy.

*Ephesians 6:11:* "Put on the whole armor of God, that you may be able to stand against the schemes of the devil."

*Ephesians 6:14–18:* "Stand therefore, having fastened on the belt of truth, and having put on the breastplate of righteousness, and, as shoes for your feet, having put on the readiness given by the gospel of peace. In all circumstances take up the shield of faith, with which you can extinguish all the flaming darts of the evil one; and take the helmet of salvation, and the sword of the

Spirit, which is the word of God, praying at all times in the Spirit, with all prayer and supplication."

Therefore, our Father provides protection over, around, underneath, and in us. He has given us the covering of His armor to protect us in spiritual warfare.

Father, how can we ever doubt Your protection? Thank You for Your protection!

May we live our lives in peace knowing that, without a doubt, we are the protected children of our Father.

## DISCUSSION QUESTIONS

1. How large are God's hands, according to Scripture?

2. How strong is God's grip?

3. What is God using to protect you today?

4. Whom has God placed around you to protect you?

5. What has God given us to wear for protection? Please explain.

6. What does Psalm 91:4 say is our protection?

7. In the same manner that God is protecting you, are you protecting your children?

## Chapter 7

# I WANT YOUR INSTRUCTION

*Proverbs 1:8:* "Hear, my son, your father's instruction."

CHILDREN ARE EMPTY VESSELS THAT WE ARE to fill with the wisdom of life. How will they learn valuable life lessons unless we share our experiences and the wisdom we obtained from them? The teaching and wisdom we share, if heeded, will prevent the future pain of failure. The teaching and wisdom that we instill in our children will set them on a course to succeed.

John Maxwell, a well-known author and speaker on the subject of leadership, once shared how his father started him on his journey of learning leadership. His father bought books dealing with subjects that would enhance leadership qualities in John. Then he paid him to read them. He also asked John to provide a written report about what he'd learned in each book.

John's father was placing valuable information in his son in a very wise manner. Is it any wonder that John has been so successful as a leader? He was ahead of the common student because he had a father guiding his learning process.

The following statistics verify that when the father is present in the learning process, the child does better in aptitude and attitude.

- Father involvement in schools is associated with the higher likelihood of a student getting mostly A's. This was true for fathers in biological-parent families, for stepfathers, and for fathers heading single-parent families.
  —Christine Winquist Nord and Jerry West, *Fathers' and Mothers' Involvement in Their Children's Schools by Family Type and Resident Status* (NCES 2001-032), Washington, D.C.: US Department of Education, National Center for Education Statistics, 2001.

If the father is not involved with the learning process, the child will struggle.

- A study assessing 4,109 two-parent families examined the effects of early maternal and paternal depression on child expressive language at age twenty-four months and the role that parent-to-child reading may play in the child's language development. The results revealed that for mothers and fathers, depressive symptoms were negatively associated with parent-to-child reading. Only for fathers, however, was earlier depression associated with later reading to child and related child expressive vocabulary development. The less the fathers read to their infants, the worse their toddler scored on a standard measure of expressive vocabulary at age two. Parents' depression has more impact on how often fathers read to their child compared to mothers, which in turn influences the child's language development.
  —J.F. Paulson, H.A. Keefe, and J.A. Leiferman, "Early Parental Depression and Child Language Development," *Journal of Child Psychology and Psychiatry*, 50, 254–262, 2009.

- Students living in father-absent homes are twice as likely to repeat a grade in school; 10 percent of children living with both parents have ever repeated a grade, compared to 20 percent of children in stepfather families and 18 percent in mother-only families.
—Christine Winquist Nord and Jerry West, *Fathers' and Mothers' Involvement in Their Children's Schools by Family Type and Resident Status* (NCES 2001-032), Washington, D.C.: US Department of Education, National Center for Education Statistics, 2001.

The Bible gives us instructions as to how and when we are to teach our children God's Word and His ways.

*Deuteronomy 11:18–20:* "You shall therefore lay up these words of mine in your heart and in your soul, and you shall bind them as a sign on your hand, and they shall be as frontlets between your eyes. You shall teach them to your children, talking of them when you are sitting in your house, and when you are walking by the way, and when you lie down, and when you rise. You shall write them on the doorposts of your house and on your gates."

- We are to teach them the Word of God until it is in their hearts.
- We are to teach them to stay focused on the Word of God.
- We are to teach them at home.
- We are to teach them when we take walks.
- We are to teach them when we retire for bed.
- We are to teach them before we start our day.
- We are to display the Word of God in prominent places in the home.

The atmosphere of our home should be filled with joy that comes from honoring God. The music, the conversation, the decorations, etc., should all contribute to the wholeness of those who live in or enter it.

The church, of course, has its place of teaching and training, but it was never intended to replace the unique teaching role of the father.

We are to teach them how to live for God. Our children need to hear the passion of our prayer. They need to hear the power of our witnessing. They must see us moved by what we read in the Bible. They must see us being the same person at home and at work that we are in church. Our children will follow what we do more than what we say.

Abraham was declared to be the father of the nation of Israel. Why?

*Genesis 18:19:* "For I have chosen him, that he may command his children and his household after him to keep the way of the Lord by doing righteousness and justice."

He would train his children to keep the way of the Lord. Abraham lived a God-conscious life, and he taught this lifestyle to his son Isaac. When God asked Abraham for the life of his son, without hesitation Abraham climbed the mount with complete determination to obey God's order. Abraham informed his servants that he and the boy were going up the mount to worship and would return. What a lesson Isaac was about to learn!

Isaac asked Abraham, "Where is the lamb?" Abraham's response was, "The Lord shall provide himself a lamb." The knife in Abraham's hand was about to plunge into his son's chest when a voice cried out, "Stop! There is a ram in the bush; offer him."

Abraham taught Isaac that *obedience is better than sacrifice.* Isaac learned that God will provide a means of salvation for the innocent to live. He learned also that worship is becoming "a living sacrifice." Worship is a lifestyle of daily obedience.

The worship our children offer to the Lord will be what we have lived and demonstrated in front of them.

As a pastor I have learned that children follow the worship style of the parents. If the parents do not sing during worship, the children do not sing. If the parents are unfaithful to God's house, so are the children. If the parents do not tithe, the children do not tithe. We become like our role model.

Moses is an example of a child who was trained in the way he should go, and when he was old he did not depart from it. Not much is said about Moses' father. His mother nursed him until he was weaned, and then she returned him to the king's daughter. Moses was so influenced in his brief upbringing that he refused to be called the son of Pharaoh's daughter. He had the word placed in him as to who he was. He was no doubt taught that he was a Jew and not an Egyptian. Could his father have taught him this? Though Moses was educated and cultured by the Egyptians, he lived out his days honoring God and the heritage of his Jewish ancestors.

*Proverbs 22:6:* "Train up a child in the way he should go; even when he is old he will not depart from it."

"Train" is *ḥanaka* in Hebrew, and means "to make experienced, submissive," as one does a horse by a rope in its mouth. The analogy of a horse with a bridle in its mouth is a picture of how discipline teaches us self-control. Discipline is learning to submit to and obey an authority figure. It is learning how to control our own spirit.

Children need an example of how life is to be lived. They are walking in our footsteps. A father, like our Heavenly Father, disciplines because he loves his child.

*Hebrews 12:6:* "For the Lord disciplines the one he loves."

As fathers, we must know that our children want to please us. When they know that they are being disciplined out of love, they will submit to it. However, a child who is disciplined without sufficient and clear explanation of the reason for the discipline becomes angry, confused, offended, and will have a broken spirit.

A father who makes demands without giving a clear explanation of his expectations creates disheartened children. His children will feel that their opinions and feelings are not respected. There is no communication. It becomes a matter of, "Because I said so!"

A good father doesn't demand more than a child can give, but he does require a certain level of responsibility from his children.

*Ephesians 6:4:* "Fathers, do not provoke your children to anger, but bring them up in the discipline and instruction of the Lord."

*Colossians 3:21:* "Fathers, do not provoke your children, lest they become discouraged."

David Bell was a teenage friend with whom I played a lot of basketball. His father was an older minister. Once when I was at his home playing basketball, I noticed that David was extremely angry and tearful. After a short time of playing basketball, he opened up to me about his issues.

He said with a growl of exasperation and frustration in his voice, "I am so angry! My dad, whenever I have done something wrong, never talks to me about it. Instead, he writes a letter and puts it on the dinner table. What kind of father is that? He makes me feel like I am not even a person."

Provoking a child can be avoided if we will only listen, teach, explain, and discipline with wisdom and love. The last thing a father ever wants to succeed at is provoking his child.

Too often, anger is beaten into a child because the father is angry when disciplining.

My father-in-law was a man I loved like a father. He was a good man, but he came from a generation that used corporal punishment at will, sometimes to an extreme. When he spanked one of his children, it was done in anger. The more he spanked, the angrier he became. His children all loved him, but they now speak openly about how his anger defeated the purpose of his discipline. It became more of a punishment than a correction.

A father should discipline after the principles taught to us by God the Father. We discover the benefits of discipline in the Book of Hebrews.

*Hebrews 12:10-11:* "For they disciplined us for a short time as it seemed best to them, but he disciplines us for our good, that we may share his holiness. For the moment all discipline seems painful rather than pleasant, but later it yields the peaceful fruit of righteousness to those who have been trained by it."

When a child is given options as to what will occur if he or she disobeys, the discipline may be avoided. The goal is to have a submissive child.

God the Father continually gave Israel choices. In Deuteronomy chapters 27 and 28, the Lord set before Israel a blessing and a curse. He made clear the consequences of disobedience and the rewards for obedience. The people would be held accountable for the choices of their behavior.

God was not seeking to punish Israel, but was giving them the choice of reward or punishment for their misbehavior. If we give our children a choice, most likely they will accept the results. They will submit to the discipline because they made the choice. They were warned. Anger will be instilled in the child when a choice is not given.

A father disciplines for the child's good. No father desires to punish his child. The heart of a father's discipline is to develop a better person.

According to the above verses, in time the fruit of discipline will be that "we share in His holiness." In other words, through discipline, a child learns right from wrong. It is painful, yes, but the dividend is a *peaceful spirit*. A child who has been trained well will be in control of his actions and attitude.

Children must know where their boundaries are. They need us to be consistent with boundaries and discipline. We must not be inconsistent with discipline.

*Proverbs 13:24:* "Whoever spares the rod hates his son, but he who loves him is diligent to discipline him."

My father trained me early in my life to respect a weapon and the rules that must be followed to ensure safety. One day, when our family was at my grandparents' house, my brother and uncle went hunting. Dad informed me that I was not allowed to go.

I became angry and argued with him. That was one spanking. I continued to push the issue. Again I was denied; again I acted out. That brought on a second spanking. Because I loved hunting, I could not imagine not going.

Not learning the lesson from the previous spankings, I slammed the front door of my grandfather's house. It should have broken out the windows, but fortunately it did not. That was spanking number three.

Not to be outdone, I locked myself inside the car so my father could not get to me—or so I thought! Unfortunately, it was a hot spring day. I could only take the heat inside the vehicle for so long. Soaking wet with sweat, I eventually got out of the car. My father was waiting. That was spanking number four.

Suddenly I came to the realization that my father knew this was not going to be a good day for hunting. I came into absolute agreement with him. I submitted to his authority. My will had been broken and placed beneath his authority.

Another reward coming from consistent discipline applied early in a child's life is that, as they grow older, it will not be as necessary. You will have not provoked them, but rather have disciplined them in love.

*Proverbs 29:17:* "Discipline your son, and he will give you rest; he will give delight to your heart."

A child who is disciplined correctly will, in time, thank his father for loving him enough to discipline him. A child who will submit to discipline will respect the orders of his boss, commander, or whatever authority figure is over him. He can take an order and finish a task. These children will not only keep a job but will be promoted, because they understand authority.

A child who does not receive discipline becomes an embarrassment to his parent.

*Proverbs 29:15:* "The rod and reproof give wisdom, but a child left to himself brings shame to his mother."

A child who will not submit to discipline will be stubborn and rebellious. He is used to having his own way. He will struggle with keeping a job, a marriage, or anything that requires self-discipline. He has not been trained to deny himself. "No" is a word he will not accept.

When I was in my early teens, I was out with some friends who had a car. We lost track of time and stayed out too late. When we realized how late it was, we fearfully and frantically started toward home. That night, we got a flat tire on the car. Places to have a flat fixed at that time of night were difficult to find. We no sooner had one repaired, when the other tire also went flat. The same process had to be repeated. We had to make two trips into town to get the flat tires fixed. Needless to say, it was very late by the time I arrived home.

I slipped into the house, hoping and praying that my dad would not be awake. Fearing the wrath of my father, I quietly tiptoed toward my room to avoid waking him. From the light outside, I saw a figure sitting in one of the living room chairs. I knew I was in trouble. It was my dad. My heart sank.

My attempts to explain my tardiness did not do away with the fact that I had started home after my curfew. Dad was holding me responsible for that decision. I was about to learn a lesson that would affect my life forever.

Dad stood up from the chair and commenced to take off his belt. Surely he was about to give me a whipping I wouldn't forget. Instead, he shocked me with his next words. He said, "Son, you are old enough now to make your own choices. I have attempted to teach you to the best of my ability. It appears that I have failed. You are too old for a spanking. I have preached to you how much Jesus loves us and went to the cross for us. He took our punishment for us. I am tired of disciplining you. I have failed you."

He placed the belt in my hand, took off his shirt, and said, "Son, you deserve a whipping, but I am going to be like Jesus and take this one for you. You whip me." He bent over the ottoman and waited for me to give him my punishment.

My heart broke. To disappoint my dad was a much worse punishment than to take a spanking. How could I ever lay a hand on my father? I cried and placed the belt back into his hand. I assured him that it would never happen again. It was a spiritual lesson that I would never forget. Jesus took my punishment that I could be saved. I never missed a curfew again.

## I WANT YOUR INSTRUCTION

If we will discipline them, we will save them from themselves. Children are not unlike Simon Peter, who argued with his Master. Being headstrong, he insisted that he would never betray the Lord. He declared that he would fight for Him to the death.

Jesus informed Simon Peter that Satan desired to sift him as wheat, but He had prayed for him that his faith would not fail. Jesus warned Peter that he would deny Him three times before the rooster crowed. As we know, it happened just as Jesus prophesied it would. As soon as the rooster crowed, Peter was instantly reminded of the warning of Jesus. The Scripture says that he went out and wept bitterly. He truly did not know what was in his heart. Now it was revealed to him. For three days, he would have to process this event. I am sure he was filled with extreme disappointment in himself. In his anguish, surely Peter must have asked himself many times how he could have betrayed the Lord.

After Jesus was resurrected, He sent word to His disciples, and specifically to Peter, to meet with Him in Galilee. In this meeting, the Lord never condemned Peter. Instead, He asked him a question to determine if he had learned a life lesson. "Peter, do you love Me?" Jesus asked.

Three times Peter had denied the Lord; now he openly confessed three times that he loved Him. Peter affirmed that he did love the Lord. He was ready for the Upper Room experience. He would be the spokesman at Pentecost when three thousand souls would believe on Jesus.

The purpose of discipline is to save someone from himself. We are indeed our own worst enemies. We must teach our children to yield their will to the will of the Master.

Discipline is intended to bring about immediate obedience to a command. It indeed may be the very action that saves a life. If a soldier in the military hesitates to obey a command, it can cost a fellow soldier his life.

**FATHER ME**

The act of our obedience is evidence of our love for Christ.

*John 14:15:* "If you love me, you will keep my commandments."

As we submit to the Father's authority, our children will submit to ours.

May we, as fathers, teach and instruct our children in the same manner our Heavenly Father has taught us.

## DISCUSSION QUESTIONS

1. According to statistics, how is a child affected if his father does not read to him?

2. How and when is a father to teach his children?

3. What are we to teach our children?

4. What is the purpose of discipline?

5. What does the phrase "train up a child" mean to you?

6. What advice would you give a young father concerning how and when to discipline his child?

7. What factors determine the form of punishment you give your child?

8. What are some of the rewards of consistent discipline?

Chapter 8

# HOW DO I REMAIN SEXUALLY PURE?

THE UNITED STATES IS FACING A SOCIAL crisis today because fathers are not giving their children a pure sexual identity. Second only to the power of the Holy Spirit, in this world, are our sexual compulsions and instincts. Our children need to have their questions answered on this subject without being condemned for the feelings and temptations they are facing. Our society is inundated with seductive messages. Billboards, television, and movies—all implement the message of being carefree, sexy, suggestive, and flirty for the purpose of connecting with the opposite sex.

In public elementary schools, children are instructed and informed about various forms of sexual expression. None of the sexual expressions taught are classified as wrong. The government takes away the responsibility of one's sexual behavior by providing abortions almost on demand. Legislation now demands that businesses provide condoms or birth control for their employees. The message is that, since you will "do it," the government will help you.

Pornography is the greatest weapon against sexual morality in America. We are number one in the world in the production of porn. Sadly, the group that is most targeted is our vulnerable teenage children. The largest group of viewers of Internet porn is children between the ages of twelve and seventeen (Family Safe Media, December 15, 2005).

Knowing that children are so exposed to misinformation and that they are naturally curious about the subject, a father must make it a personal goal to teach his children to become godly and pure witnesses for Jesus.

What can a father do to protect his children from sexual vulnerability?

## Secure the Environment of Your Home as Much as Possible

Rid the home of any television or programming that does not support the values you desire to teach your children. Many Christians today are moving away from satellite and network programming to content that is more family-oriented and controlled, such as Netflix, Internet television, or select DVDs. Do not permit pornography in your home.

## Be Attentive to Their Friends

Know who their friends are and the moral values of the homes that they are being reared in.

*1 Corinthians 15:33:* "Do not be deceived: Bad company ruins good morals."

Be careful regarding those you allow your children to spend the night with—even family. It only takes one event to destroy your child's sexual wholeness.

## Establish Dating Rules

I would suggest the first rule to be considered would be not to allow them to date non-Christians. When I was a teenager, there were many young ladies I wanted to date, but I didn't. Sometimes they'd ask me for dates, and I gave them phony answers. I never dated non-Christian young ladies, because I knew when I told Dad I had a date, the first questions he'd ask would be, "Is she a Christian? Does she love Jesus? Where does she attend church?"

My father had a biblical basis for being so guarded about whom I dated.

*2 Corinthians 6:14:* "Do not be unequally yoked with unbelievers. For what partnership has righteousness with lawlessness? Or what fellowship has light with darkness?"

If our children are allowed to date a person who is not a Christian, we increase the odds of them marrying such a person. If that occurs, immediately their home will be divided concerning family values, discipline of children, and what form of religious training those children will receive. It is highly possible that a parent will pay a sorrowful price in the future for allowing a child to become involved with an unbeliever. Your son or daughter might raise your grandchildren with an entirely different attitude toward moral issues and God, simply because of a marriage decision.

God warned the people of Israel not to marry those who did not worship their God. They were warned that, in the end, their children and grandchildren would turn from God and worship idols. That indeed was the outcome. How many times have you witnessed a family grieve the fact that their child was not raising his or her children with the Christian principles that they themselves were taught?

There is no guarantee that marrying a Christian will not bring its own issues, but the odds greatly increase that the couple will remain true to one another because their parents modeled staying together. Children of divorce, divorce. Children brought up in a family without divorce are more likely to stay together.

Other rules should include the accountability you expect from them such as the time to be home, places that are off limits, whom they will be with, etc. These rules of course should be explained completely to both parties before the date.

Once the guidelines are established they should then be strictly and consistently enforced.

## Give Them a Way Out

Always provide a child with a means of communication to contact you when he or she deems it necessary. Emergencies such as accidents, a sense of danger, delays because of unexpected events, or a change of plans will occur. A parent will rest much easier when they are easily notified.

A young man in our church called and asked his parents to pick him up at a specific location because the environment had drastically changed. It was violating his conscience. I gave him public recognition for doing the right thing and bringing honor to his parents by calling them.

## Check Electronic Communications

Check the messages on their phones as well as content on computers. Predators and smut peddlers will attempt to pull them into tantalizing websites and draw them into a trap. With the introduction of Smartphones, inappropriate photos are easy to exchange. If your children know that you are checking their data, it will certainly hinder their participation and protect them from such traps.

## Teach Modesty

Monitor the attire your children wear so that their clothing supports a testimony of purity. Teach them the importance of respecting their own bodies. The body is to be used for God's glory, because it is His temple. The body is to be respected by dressing it in modest clothing.

If you are a father of a daughter, you know the fashions or styles that attract a man's attention. It is your responsibility to teach your daughter what is or is not acceptable.

*1 Timothy 2:9:* "Likewise also that women should adorn themselves in respectable apparel, with modesty and self-control."

If you are the father of a son, you should teach him that he is to look upon a woman as a sister (1 Timothy 5:2). Also, consult with your wife, and together point out to him how a son should dress in various public situations, as well as in the home. We must be honorable about how we present ourselves.

## Avoid Temptation

The Word of God gives us instruction on how to avoid sexual temptation. If our instruction about sexual issues is to be taken seriously, we must teach our children from the Word of God itself. With the Bible as a guide, God becomes the voice of absolute authority.

*Proverbs 6:23–24:* "For the commandment is a lamp and the teaching a light, and the reproofs of discipline are the way of life, to preserve you from the evil woman."

The Book of Proverbs contains many stories of a father warning his son concerning sexual attraction and the opposite sex. We are all sexual persons. We all have sexual urges and temptations. There is nothing wrong with being tempted, but it is wrong to live with the temptation. You can be tempted without sinning. Here are a few ways to stay strong.

***1. Run away when you are tempted.*** Put distance between you and the person who is tempting you! Isn't that what Joseph did? He left his outer cloak with Potiphar's wife and ran out of the house. Distance is indeed a safety factor. Too much togetherness breaks down walls of resistance. It becomes easier and easier to venture into forbidden physical contact.

Paul gives clear instruction on what we should do when tempted.

*2 Timothy 2:22:* "So flee youthful passions and pursue righteousness, faith, love, and peace, along with those who call on the Lord from a pure heart."

**2. Don't touch inappropriately.** The sin of Eve in the Garden was that, after being warned by God, she touched the forbidden fruit. Touching creates passion.

*Proverbs 5:20:* "Why should you be intoxicated, my son, with a forbidden woman and embrace the bosom of an adulteress?"

*Proverbs 6:27:* "Can a man carry fire next to his chest and his clothes not be burned?"

There is danger in an inappropriate kiss.

*Proverbs 5:3:* "For the lips of a forbidden woman drip honey."

Jesus uses a hyperbole to make a point concerning being tempted to touch.

*Matthew 5:30:* "If your right hand causes you to sin, cut it off and throw it away. For it is better that you lose one of your members than that your whole body go into hell."

Jesus uses the exaggeration of severing a hand to avoid carrying out the desire of our lust or temptation.

**3. Don't look.** The Holy Spirit gave me a wonderful truth recently. He said, "Never place in front of you what you don't want in you." Beware of what you allow yourself to view.

*Proverbs 4:25:* "Let your eyes look directly forward, and your gaze be straight before you."

The message of the wanting is found in the eyes. Avoid the licentious stare that says, "I want you." It is the stare of lust.

*Proverbs 6:25:* "Do not desire her beauty in your heart, and do not let her capture you with her eyelashes."

Jesus explains how lust is connected to the eye in His teaching in Matthew 5:28, "But I say to you that everyone who looks at a woman with lustful intent has already committed adultery with her in his heart."

Notice He did not say, "He who looks at *women* has committed adultery." The focus has narrowed to "a woman." When you have focused with lust on the attraction of one woman, it becomes the same as adultery in the heart.

Jesus continues His radical teaching concerning the temptation of touching:

*Matthew 5:29:* "If your right eye causes you to sin, tear it out and throw it away. For it is better that you lose one of your members than that your whole body be thrown into hell."

Again, this is a hyperbole. It is an exaggeration to make a point. Sever or separate yourself from access to fulfill your desire.

King David brought a curse upon his family because he looked upon Bathsheba from the roof of his house and saw her naked, bathing herself. Then he was not satisfied until he had her for himself.

What you focus on reveals what is in your heart.

**4. Don't converse with a promiscuous person.** Every relationship begins with conversation. Whenever the conversation turns toward you being the object of fulfilling that person's sexual desire, put an abrupt end to that conversation. State, with a stern warning, that you are not one who entertains such conversation.

*Proverbs 4:24:* "Put away from you crooked speech, and put devious talk far from you."

*Proverbs 5:3–4:* "For the lips of a forbidden woman drip honey, and her speech is smoother than oil, but in the end she is bitter as wormwood, sharp as a two-edged sword."

**5. Fill your heart with the Word of God.** Because our hearts are filled with the Word of the Lord, we desire to please Him. Isn't this what was in the heart of Joseph when the lady of the house grabbed his coat and demanded that he sleep with her? He said, "How then can I do this great wickedness and sin against God?" (Genesis 39:9)

*Proverbs 4:23:* "Keep your heart with all vigilance, for from it flow the springs of life."

*Psalm 119:9–11:* "How can a young man keep his way pure? By guarding it according to your word. With my whole heart I seek you; let me not wander from your commandments! I have stored up your word in my heart, that I might not sin against you."

## The Dangers of Impurity

If we guard our hearts, we can overcome temptation. In fact, to the pure heart, sexual advancement and aggressiveness is an offense. Preparing the hearts of our children to walk in purity requires that we warn them of why God forbids sex outside of the marriage covenant. Here are some reasons to remain pure.

**1. Self-worth is affected because of loss of sexual innocence.** The devil will use this loss of innocence to speak lies about you—to tell you that you are "used merchandise" or that you should continue in your sin to get what you want.

**2. Look forward to your wedding vows.** When you exchange vows with your future spouse and are married, there will be no remorse that you were a virgin.

**3. Avoid the comparison trap.** After you are married, the devil can use your lack of innocence as a wedge. He can use your carnal knowledge against you to create dissatisfaction with your mate.

My uncle Jody was a man of the Word and was full of wisdom. I will never forget his telling me, "Glenn, I work with men who have experienced several relationships. Their conversation is filled with dissatisfaction. I thank God that I was a virgin when I married, because I have no one to compare my wife with."

Men who do not serve the Lord view women as a prize or a challenge to be won. They think that sex is only physical in nature. To them it is just an act. They take pride in the number of women they have taken.

When sex occurs, a soul tie is established between the partners, whether they are married or not. It is an emotional connection. There is an exchange of spirit that takes place. When established outside of marriage, it is an open door to future temptation that the devil can use against you.

Comparison will lead to dissatisfaction, and that can make you vulnerable to repeated temptation.

**4. Past sexual relationships outside of marriage can create distrust in the marriage.** Jealousy will surface because you had sex before marriage. It is especially so if you have had sex with your spouse before marriage. Your companion may see you having a conversation with a person of the opposite sex that is perfectly innocent. Yet when you laugh, the devil says to your spouse, "He or she is flirting with that person. If he had sex with you before marriage, how do you know that he will not cheat on you after marriage?"

**5. The most obvious danger, of course, is contracting a social disease.** One is indeed taking a risk with the unknown. You never know the secrets or personal life of the person you are drawn to. The wise man Solomon warned us of this.

*Proverbs 5:8–11:* "Keep your way far from her, and do not go near the door of her house, lest you give your honor to others and your years to the merciless, lest strangers take their fill of your strength, and your labors go to the house of a foreigner, and at the end of your life you groan, when your flesh and body are consumed."

The following statistics, according to the American Sexual Health Association, verify the dangers of contracting a social disease.

- More than half of all people will have an STD/STI at some point in their lifetime.
- Recent estimates from the Centers for Disease Control and Infection show that there are 19.7 million new STIs every year in the United States.
- Fewer than half of adults ages eighteen to forty-four have ever been tested for an STD/STI other than HIV/AIDS.
- Each year, one in four teens contracts an STD/STI.
- One in two sexually active persons will contract an STD/STI by age twenty-five.

**6. The person who indulges in fornication or adultery loses his sense of good judgment.** Proverbs 6:32 says, "He who commits adultery lacks sense; he who does it destroys himself."

Why would a man or a woman walk out on a child and a mate they have committed themselves to? They have lost their sense of judgment. They are blinded by false love and infatuation for another person. It is an abnormal and unnatural desire. Natural desire is for our children and mate.

Proverbs describes the mind-set of such a person with the word *intoxicated*.

*Proverbs 5:20:* "Why should you be intoxicated, my son, with a forbidden woman?"

Intoxication implies that one is excited or exhilarated to the point of losing control of his or her faculties or behavior. They are not themselves. They have lost all sense of good judgment. This will lead to a hard heart. The hard heart is calloused to the cost, loss, or injury to other people affected by their behaviors.

Solomon predicts the end result of such behavior.

*Proverbs 6:33:* "He will get wounds and dishonor, and his disgrace will not be wiped away."

Great men who have experienced public knowledge of sexual transgression are not remembered for all the good they accomplished. Instead, they are remembered for their moral failure. King David was a man after God's own heart, but his tryst with Bathsheba followed him to his grave.

## The Rewards of Purity

While we must inform our children of the dangers of sexual impurity, we must also emphasize the positive aspects of purity. The wise father will continually point out to his children the rewards that come from being a virgin until they give themselves in marriage. We must teach them that sex is holy, good, and pure in marriage.

*Hebrews 13:4 (NKJV):* "Marriage is honorable among all, and the bed undefiled; but fornicators and adulterers God will judge."

Therefore, sex outside of marriage is sin.

The best reason to maintain sexual purity is for the purpose of having maximum pleasure with our mate. Sex must not be presented as something dirty but rather as something holy. It is intended to be pleasurable and should be restricted solely to the marriage relationship.

The rewards that come to the sexually pure are the following:

**1. The virtuous person, when he or she marries, will enjoy ultimate trust from the mate.** Virginity is proof that you are worthy to be honored.

**2. The virtuous person will enjoy a special bonding that comes only from God.** A person who enters the marriage relationship with purity and virginity will have the reward of experiencing God's indescribable blessing in the relationship.

*Genesis 2:24 (KJV):* "Therefore shall a man leave his father and his mother, and shall cleave unto his wife: and they shall be one flesh."

The word *cleave* in Hebrew is a word for "glue." This is the bond that God desires to add to the marriage. It is an "until death do us part" kind of glue.

*Mark 10:9:* "What therefore God has joined together, let not man separate."

The marriage union is one that God honors. There are severe penalties for attempting to divide a union established by God.

**3. The virtuous person will have the satisfaction of knowing they have pleased God.** The virtuous person will live with no remorse, regret, or guilt. They are free to enjoy the innocence of the wondrous design of God for loving a companion, without anything being hidden.

### 4. The virtuous person honors his or her parents, and in return will receive honor.

Parents are honored by the integrity, self-discipline, and obedience of a child that has lived a pure life before God and man. A child that has lived a life that has honored the parents will receive the honor of God.

### 5. The virtuous person will not bring a sexual disease to the marriage partner.

Virtue is expected to be continued into the marriage relationship. The Christian view of marriage is that it is not a contract but a covenant. Contracts may be broken or altered but a covenant is for life. It is for the purpose of committing ourselves by a vow that we will be faithful to one another till death.

The person who is a virgin will not be responsible for bringing a sexual disease into the marriage.

Jesus chose the image of a virgin to describe His Church. She is seen as being clothed in righteousness, purity, and without spot or wrinkle. We are to live our lives with the ultimate goal of living holy, waiting for the arrival of Jesus to take us to the Marriage Supper of the Lamb. The best of heaven is reserved for the Bride.

In the same way, the best is reserved for those who save themselves in purity for their spouse.

## DISCUSSION QUESTIONS

1. As a father, what are some safeguards that you have in place to protect your children from being sexually violated?

2. What standards do you have for whom your children will or will not be allowed to date?

3. What biblical truths can you give your children that will help them to avoid sexual temptation?

4. Why does God condemn sex outside of the marriage covenant?

5. What are some penalties for sexual sin?

6. What are the rewards of being a virgin at the time of marriage?

Chapter 9

# WILL YOU GIVE ME A FATHER'S BLESSING?

IT IS THE INTENTION OF GOD THAT each generation be blessed by the previous generation. God established a generational covenant with Abraham. When God identified himself commonly in the Old Testament, He did so by saying, "I am the God of Abraham, Isaac, and Jacob." The blessing of the covenant was passed on.

Whatever God initiated in Scripture, He institutes by the role of the father-son relationship. Physical as well as spiritual fatherhood brought generational blessings on those to whom they were imparted. Some examples are the kings in the lineage of King David, the Levite descendants who served in the temple, leadership such as Moses to Joshua, and the prophet's mantle, passed from Elijah to Elisha. Each ministry of service had a transferable blessing.

The priesthood descended in each generation from Aaron. Each time a new priest was ordained, he wore the already-anointed garments of his father. Fresh anointing oil was then poured on those garments again to honor his role as a priest. What we see is that God intended the following generation to walk in greater favor and blessing than the previous.

When kings were established, it was expected that a son would take the throne of his father. A son was to build on the foundation of the past father's reign.

Every father should desire to lay a foundation that his offspring can value and build upon. A father wills his children to live longer, become more successful, be better educated, increase the family wealth, and enjoy a better life than he had.

A father can bless his children with a good name. The Bible says in Proverbs 22:1, "A good name is to be chosen rather than great riches."

It is difficult to overcome a bad family name. My father was opening the car door for his date when her father abruptly showed up. He grabbed his daughter by the arm and snatched her out of the car. He said to her, "What do you think you are doing? That young man is a Dorsey! Dorseys are no good. You can never see him again."

My grandfather was an abusive alcoholic. He was a poor sharecropper with a large family. His reputation preceded him. When he became drunk, his actions were known throughout the community.

Our family name was dramatically blessed when my father gave his life to Christ. I never heard him swear. I never witnessed him lay a hand on my mother. Alcohol and tobacco were not allowed in our home. My father always had a good credit rating and paid his bills on time. Dad was a man of integrity.

At a special meeting in Dublin, Ireland, I was teaching and demonstrating the emotional healing process to the leaders of the Assemblies of God of Ireland. While I was presenting a special part about the father's blessing, Sean Malarkey, pastor of St. Mark's, was visibly moved. At the end of the presentation, he came to me and said, "Glenn, you don't know the impact of this blessing on the Irish culture. During the presentation of the father's blessing, I took your words personally, and they impacted me. What you don't understand about Ireland is that we have large families, and because of work, often the father is absent from the home. When he is not working, he is at the pub. What we have is a generation that is seeking their father's blessing." I have not forgotten what he said.

The need remains the same, regardless of the country you live in. We have a generation that is desperate for a father's blessing.

The first recorded blessing of a father to his son in the Bible is God the Father to Adam.

*Genesis 1:28:* "And God blessed them. And God said to them, 'Be fruitful and multiply and fill the earth and subdue it, and have dominion over the fish of the sea and over the birds of the heavens and over every living thing that moves on the earth.'"

The second recorded blessing is from God the Father to His son Noah and his sons.

*Genesis 9:1:* "And God blessed Noah and his sons and said to them, 'Be fruitful and multiply and fill the earth.'"

The third recorded blessing is from God the Father to Abram.

*Genesis 12:1–2:* "Now the Lord said to Abram, 'Go from your country and your kindred and your father's house to the land that I will show you. And I will make of you a great nation, and I will bless you and make your name great, so that you will be a blessing.'"

Isaac, in Genesis 27, is the first man recorded to bless his son. It is a pattern that would be passed on in the family as a generational blessing.

Fathers have the power to bless or curse with their words. We can label our children or verbally abuse them, and they will live out the words we have spoken over them.

Isaac named one of his sons Jacob. Jacob means "supplanter or deceiver." He lived out the label his father had given him.

*Genesis 27:36:* "Esau said, 'Is he not rightly named Jacob? For he has cheated me these two times. He took away my birthright, and behold, now he has taken away my blessing.'"

One of the definitions for blessing is "the formal act of approving." In other words, you bless a person with words that you desire for their future, so that God can bless them.

When a father speaks a blessing over his children, he is giving them favor to pursue their dreams and visions. My father was constantly blessing my brother and me. He would tell us that we could become anything we desired to be. Often in my life, people have mistaken my self-confidence for arrogance. It was not arrogance. It was a father's blessing spoken over me that I believed. Because my father believed in me, I believed in myself. I believed I could do whatever Dad said I could do.

A dear friend of mine shared his personal story with me. He told me of a recent breakthrough he'd had with his father. His father was sick and elderly, so he moved him into his home to care for him. His father was one of the angriest men I had ever met. He could be very kind and caring, but you never knew when he would explode in anger. It had been a personal problem for years.

The Holy Spirit spoke to my friend James and said, "You need to go home, so you can go home." He knew exactly what that meant. He knew that if he did not seek to reconcile with his father before he died, he would never have peace. He knew that his father would not come to him, so he went home to where his father was. He needed to let go of his past and embrace what precious moments he had left with his father. He needed both to forgive his father and to seek forgiveness from his father.

With tears welling up in his eyes, James said, "Glenn, I bowed on my knees in front of my sick father and told him, Dad, I am in my late fifties, and all of my life I have been afraid of you, and that is not right. From the time I was a small boy, and even after you were saved, you have carried this anger. You let go of the alcohol and all the other evil vices, but you have kept your anger. When you become angry, it causes me to return to the past, and fear overwhelms me."

"All of my life I have tried to please you, and I have never been good enough. I have five degrees, but that hasn't been enough to gain your favor. There is something that happened to me when I was a boy that I could not tell you, because I didn't know how you would respond to me. When you were out of town working, a neighbor molested me. Daddy, I have struggled with my own anger and never feeling good enough because of what happened to me. Dad, I need you to do something for me before you die: forgive me. And I want to forgive you of everything. I need you to bless me."

His father was wise enough to know what needed to be done at that moment. He asked James for his forgiveness, and then he reached out a hand, placed it on his head, and began to speak a blessing over him. He told him how proud he was of his accomplishments and of the people he had helped. He spoke blessing over his future and his family.

James said, "Glenn, at that moment, the fear that I'd lived with most of my life was instantly broken. The fear went away. The rest of the time that I had with my father until he died—they were some of the best moments of my life."

This is the power of a father's blessing.

# FATHER ME

You may be asking yourself, "How can I bless my child? I don't know what to say." Allow me to assist you.

One of the most treasured memories I have as a father is when I blessed my son. I planned a special day just to be with him for the purpose of blessing him.

We played a men's golf tournament together, and he had a great time. I then took him to the nicest steakhouse in town and allowed him to order whatever he wanted. When he finished his meal, I began to speak into his life what he meant to me and how I believed in him and his future.

I made it a practice to do this on more than one occasion, and I was specific with my blessing. I love being a father!

I suggest that you plan a very special moment to impact your children with a father's blessing. It should come at a time in their lives when you feel it will mean the most to them. Do something with your children that they really enjoy doing with you, whatever that is. Then take your children to a special private place that they will not forget—a place that you know will wow them. When you are alone and there is no opportunity for interruption or distraction, tell your child the reason you planned this time together.

Stand in front of him with your hands on his head and begin to bless him.

The following is a general pattern that you can follow to speak a life-changing blessing over your child. Of course, make it gender-relative.

> I am your father. I want to express to you how important you are to me. I want to speak a blessing over you and your future.
>
> I love you.

## WILL YOU GIVE ME A FATHER'S BLESSING?

I bless you with my unconditional love. There is nothing you can do that will ever cause me to love you more or to love you less.

I am not ashamed to call you my child. I am so proud of you.

I bless you with access to me at any time you need it, day or night. I bless you with my presence. Whenever you need me, I will be there for you. I promise that I will never leave or abandon you, emotionally or physically. You are so important to me that I don't want to miss any important events in your life.

I do not expect perfection from you. Failure is permitted. You will only learn from failing how to succeed. When you were learning to walk, you fell repeatedly. I was there to pick you up and encourage you to try again. If you fail at something, as your father, I will always be there to help pick you up and help get you back on course.

I bless you with the determination to succeed. I believe in you. I bless you with the favor of God to succeed according to Psalm 1:3—you will be like a tree planted by the rivers of water; you will bring forth fruit in due season and your leaf will not fade or wither; everything you do will prosper."

I bless you to be the head and not the tail.

I bless you to pursue the will of God, to pursue your dreams, to have great visions and personal goals. Psalm 37:4, "Delight yourself in the Lord and he will give you the desire of your heart."

I bless you with provision. I will provide for your necessities to the best of my ability. I offer you all my resources to help you reach for the stars, as long as you are willing to make the effort.

I bless you with my protection. I will protect you from any enemy and, if necessary, with God's help, I will die in the effort.

I bless you with courage to live life with a continued faith in a loving God.

I bless you with health. I bless you with a sound mind.

I bless you with the freedom to become whatever the Father wills you to be. I bless you with your own identity. You are not who people say you are. You are not who you think you are. You are who I say you are. I say you are good, brilliant, loving, talented, gifted, and uncommon.

I say that you are mine, and I love you!

When you speak these words over your child, make them your words and speak the blessing you bestow upon them from your heart.

The concept that your children have of God will be based on the relationship that they have with you as their father. They call you father. When they pray "Our Father," they will identify with Him based on your relationship with them.

Your children are longing for a moment like this. Give it to them.

Not only do we seek our father's blessing, but we should also desire our Heavenly Father's blessing. The Father desires to bless you! Live your life for Christ, knowing you have His favor and blessing.

## DISCUSSION QUESTIONS

1. How important is a good family name?

2. Who was the first person to receive his father's blessing in the Bible?

3. Who was the first father who spoke a blessing over his son in the Bible?

4. Did your father speak a blessing over you? If so, share it. If he did not, share what it would have meant to you to hear him speak one over you.

5. Will you plan a time to give your child your special blessing?

Chapter 10

# PREPARE ME TO LIVE INDEPENDENTLY OF YOU

**I** READ AN ARTICLE RECENTLY, WRITTEN BY A mother who was teaching her son how to swim. It impacted me deeply. God spoke to her in that setting about her role as a parent. It was a powerful word. This is how she explained it.

> *"I would have let him go one finger at a time, until, without his realizing, he'd be floating without me. And then I thought, perhaps that is what it means to be a [parent]—to teach your child to live without you."*
>
> —Nicole Krauss

What is God's life assignment for your child's future? Have your children been given to you to relive your dreams through them, or to fulfill His will for their lives?

Of course, as Christian fathers, we want God's best for our children. Our greatest assignment as fathers is to prepare our children to hit the target that God has for their lives. This is illustrated for us in the Psalms with the powerful image of an arrow.

*Psalm 127:4–5:* "Like arrows in the hand of a warrior are the children of one's youth. Blessed is the man who fills his quiver with them! He shall not be put to shame when he speaks with his enemies in the gate."

What are children compared to in these verses? Arrows? If children are like arrows, we need to know more about an arrow to increase our understanding of the symbolism. This is what I have learned about arrows that I feel will help us understand this picture better for life applications.

## Children, Like Arrows, Must Be Straight to Hit the Target

The Word of God placed in a child will ensure that the child will know the right paths to take in life. A child will live out the truth that has been instilled in him and demonstrated by his father. Though we have them but for a short time, the Word that we place in them will influence them for the rest of their lives.

*Proverbs 22:6:* "Train up a child in the way he should go; even when he is old he will not depart from it."

Recently I asked people to write the name of the person who had influenced them the most in becoming a lifetime follower of Jesus Christ on a public display at the church. I also asked them to bring a childhood picture of themselves. During the message that morning, I pointed out that the picture they displayed from their childhood and the person's name they posted as the most influential person in their Christian lives should speak a message to them. The message is, "You are here today as a much older person because someone put the Word of God in you." You, at one time, were the arrow in someone's hand.

## A Crooked Arrow Will Never Hit Its Mark

> *"A single action can cause a life to veer off in a direction it was never meant to go."*
> —Anita Shreve

A father can disrupt the good path a child is taking by making a bad decision that destroys his child's confidence in him as a father. It can mess up the child for life. We must be reminded that we must live a life before them that they will desire to follow. We must make good choices with our own lives.

A teacher can determine, quite readily, when a child is not being well prepared for life. The earmarks of such a child may be that he or she is indecisive, restless, insecure, confused, timid, withdrawn, rebellious, without understanding of moral values, angry, and fearful. These children are victims of parents neglecting the need of preparing for their future. They are being raised without purpose or instruction about life.

## An Arrow That Hits the Target Must Have a Spine

The stiffness of the shaft is known as its *spine*, referring to how little the shaft bends when compressed. Hence, an arrow that bends less is said to have more spine.

We want our children to be strong-willed and determined. We desire that they be finishers and completers of their life assignments. When the arrow is in the bow and is released, it must have the strength to withstand the power of thrust that is placed upon it. It remains straight under pressure.

## Children, Like Arrows, Must Have Suppleness When They Hit the Target

Suppleness means to have flexibility. The arrow must not shatter; it should be reusable. While we want our children to be strong-willed, focused, and self-confident, we must also teach them the importance of humility.

When they hit the mark, we want them to know that they have succeeded by the grace of God. Their success does not mean that they are better than others, but that they have been properly placed and trained for their assignment, while others have not.

## Children, Like Arrows, Need to Be "Footed"

Sometimes a shaft will be made of two different types of wood fastened together, resulting in what is known as a "footed" arrow. Footed arrows typically consist of a short length of hardwood near the head of the arrow, with the remainder of the shaft consisting of softwood.

Because the area most likely to break has been reinforced, the arrow is more likely to survive impact while still maintaining overall flexibility and lighter weight.

We must prepare our children for the hard knocks of life—the realities of life. The Christian life can be one of tribulation as well as persecution. Because we know the child's weaknesses, we reinforce those areas. We build up the areas of weakness in the child for difficult times in his or her future.

For example:

- If the child is fearful, we will teach her to practice the presence of the Father.

- If he is rebellious, we instruct and discipline him for the purpose of teaching him to control his own spirit.
- If she is selfish, we teach her the joy of sharing and giving.
- If he is prideful, we teach him the power of humility.
- If she compares herself to others, we build up her uniqueness as a person.

## Children, Like Arrows, Must Be Balanced to Hit the Target

We want to avoid teaching them extremisms. Perhaps a better word would be to avoid prejudices.

A balanced life will avoid the following prejudices:

- Racial prejudice: We are many races but one people. God has made us all of the same blood.
- Financial prejudice: Wealth, or a lack of it, does not do away with the responsibility that we are to love one another.
- Gender prejudice: Men and women are equal in the kingdom of God.
- Denominational prejudice: Our differences are to be respected, but our Jesus is to be shared.

## Children, Like Arrows, Need Fletching

Fletching are feathers found at the back of the arrow that act as airfoils to provide a small amount of force that stabilizes the flight of the arrow.

A feather that a father might add to stabilize the future course of a child could be teaching him or her the value of character. Honesty, faithfulness, being on time, trusting, being thankful, being a person of their word, patience—all these are character traits that will assist our children in hitting their mark.

Another feather that can stabilize the future of a child is teaching him or her the value of a daily routine. Show me a person's daily routine, and I will predict his future. One thing a person of wealth values that a poor man does not is time. What we do each day determines whether we hit the mark or not.

The feather of boundaries being in place will give them a sense of safety. A child must know the limits that are in place that he cannot violate without repercussion. Rules should be for betterment, not penalty. Time will prove to your children that you were for them, not against them.

> *"You spend years wishing your parents would get off your back, only to realize that they are the only ones who ever had your back."*
> —*Author unknown*

## Children, Like Arrows, Will Be in Our Hands but for a Short Time

There is not a father who loves his children who does not understand the feelings that Job describes in the following verses.

*Job 29:2,4–5:* "Oh, that I were as in the months of old, as in the days when God watched over me…as I was in my prime, when the friendship of God was upon my tent, when the Almighty was yet with me, when my children were all around me."

Time passes so quickly. We must be diligent in redeeming the time we have with these precious lives. It is easy to become distracted with the business of life and neglect those precious early years of our children. I have yet to hear a father say, "I wish I had not spent so much time with my kids." The opposite of that statement is true.

## Children, Like Arrows in the Hand, Must Be Aimed at the Right Target

We can ill afford to allow our children to find their own way. If we do, they will live a very unsettled life.

*Proverbs 29:15:* "But a child left to himself brings shame to his mother."

They must have the help of their father to be guided in the right direction. We must know where God is taking them. The command of Proverbs 22:6 is the same—"Train up a child in the way he should go." Don't leave him to himself.

When an arrow is "in hand," that means it is about to be released. This implies that we are to help guide their course, their future! As fathers, we should know how to get the best out of our children. In order to do this, we must know how to meet the emotional needs of the child.

## Five Critical Emotional Needs of Children

Emotional health provides a solid foundation for success in school, work, marriage, and life in general. Failure to recognize and satisfy these five needs jeopardizes the future of our children and of succeeding generations.

**1. The Need to Feel Respected.** If we want children to grow up feeling respected and treating others with respect, we need to:

- Avoid sarcasm, belittling, and yelling.
- Keep anger and impatience to a minimum.
- Avoid lying.
- Listen more and talk less.

- Learn how to say please, thank you, excuse me, and I'm sorry—yes, even to children.

We need to become conscious of our own mistakes, willing to admit them, and ready to make corrections. This will help us cultivate these values in our children.

**2. *The Need to Feel Important or Valued.*** This need is evident at a very early age. Children want to know that you notice they are in the room. They want you to notice the A on the grade card. They seek your affirmation of their accomplishments—even if they are just tiptoeing to turn on a light switch or tying their shoes.

Children want to do things for themselves, and so often we get in their way. As fathers, we must avoid being all powerful—solving all family problems, making all of the decisions, doing all the work, controlling everything that happens.

Children want to be involved. Ask their opinions, give them things to do, share decision making and power, give them status and recognition, and have patience with mistakes or when it takes a little longer or is not done as well as you could have done yourself.

If children do not feel important—if they don't develop a sense of value in constructive ways—they may seek negative ways to get attention, to feel that they are "somebody."

**3. *The Need to Feel Accepted.*** Children need to feel accepted as individuals in their own right, with their own uniqueness. They should not be compared to siblings or anyone else. To compare them immediately implies that they are not good enough.

They will feel accepted when they have the right to claim their own feelings, opinions, concerns, wants, needs, and dreams. Trivializing, ignoring, or ridiculing a child's feelings or opinions is a rejection that weakens the relationship. Paying attention to and discussing their opinions and feelings, even when you do not like or disagree with some of them, strengthens the relationship.

*4. The Need to Feel Included.* Children need to be brought in, to be made to feel a part of things, to feel connected to other people, to have a sense of community. This happens when people engage with others in activities and projects, and when they experience things together in a meaningful way. It is important for the family to create these opportunities.

People who do things together feel closer to one another. Family activities offer a way to become closer and also to have fun, learn, and contribute to others.

*5. The Need to Feel Secure.* Children flourish in an environment that is positive. They accomplish more when jealousy and envy are not permitted. Don't ask them to compete with others in the family. Celebrate their differences and not their likenesses to family members. Encourage them to be their unique selves.

## Children, Like Arrows in the Hand, Are Chosen for a Specific Purpose

Some arrows serve for target practice, others for hunting, and yet others for war. The same is true with each child. They are gifted for specific purposes.

Here are a few names from the Bible that are synonymous with specific life assignments.

- Samson was a deliverer.
- Samuel was a prophet.
- David was a warrior, songwriter, leader, and king.

- Noah was a shipbuilder.
- Asaph was a choir director.
- Joseph and Daniel were politicians.
- Dorcas made coats and clothes for widows.
- Adam was a farmer.
- Esther was an intercessor to the king for the Jewish people.

A "life assignment" means that God gave them life for a specific purpose and task.

We must make our children aware that, because of their life assignments, the enemy will attack them. It is imperative that we alert them to conflicts that they will face in establishing their calling and purpose. The enemy will attempt to detour them from their life purpose. He will offer many opportunities to turn them away from their destiny. They will struggle and perhaps even suffer on their way to placement. Success has a costly price connected to it.

- Samson may have been a deliverer, but he was always outnumbered in battle.
- Samuel may have been a prophet, but he was disappointed with the desire of the people for a king.
- David—warrior, songwriter, and leader—lived in caves. Five times, his father-in-law Saul threw a javelin at him, trying to kill him. His own men became so discouraged in battle that they, too, considered taking David's life. In spite of all this conflict and struggle, however, David fulfilled his life assignment and became king!
- Noah was a shipbuilder, but he was mocked for doing a new thing.
- Joseph and Daniel faced jail time and the threat of death for fulfilling their life assignments.
- Dorcas made coats and clothes for widows, yet faced death herself.
- Adam was a farmer, but he dealt with the devil head-on.

## PREPARE ME TO LIVE INDEPENDENTLY OF YOU

A father must allow his children to experience hard knocks. Because a father provides for a child's needs, it is easy for children to buy into the idea of "easy come, easy go."

> *"After their children are grown and gone, many a parent realizes that for all their good intentions, they have handicapped the children they love more than life. They have damaged them, not out of cruelty but out of kindness. By giving their children all they could ever need or want, they have deprived them of the very things God uses to make us into the men and women He has called us to be."*
> —Richard Exley

It isn't until a child *experience*s the cost that he understands there *is* a cost.

*Romans 5:3–4, (NIV):* "We know that suffering produces perseverance; perseverance, character; and character, hope."

Isn't this what we want our children to be?

Training up a child who will have these traits in his or her life does not come without skill on our part. "I shot an arrow into the air; it fell to earth I know not where," will be the words of a father who is living his life without the focus of his children's future in mind. The young people we desire to see develop into outstanding, mature, and productive persons will only become that way because we made their successful release a priority in our life. They will only hit the target of their life assignment because we practiced the time of their release.

*Psalm 127:3 (NKJV):* "Behold, children are a heritage from the LORD, the fruit of the womb is a reward. Like arrows in the hand of a warrior, so are the children of one's youth."

Do you see it? An arrow in the hand of a warrior! The picture reveals that the life of a child has been placed in the hand of a person with experience and skill.

When I was in elementary school, a professional archer presented a demonstration. I sat in awe of his skill as he cut cards in half, hit moving targets, and even shot an apple while he was blindfolded. How was he able to perform such unusual feats? He had released so many arrows that he learned how to hit his target. His practice assured him of his skill to release and hit the target in public view.

We practice releasing in life in stages.

- The first time they walk.
- The first time we leave them with a babysitter.
- The first time they ride a bicycle.
- The first day they go to school.
- The first time they shoot a weapon.
- The first time they drive a car.
- The first time they go out on a date.
- The first day you leave them at their college dorm.
- The day you witness them take their wedding vows.

Because you are aware of the talent, interest, calling, or life assignment your child has, you have invested time and money in developing it. You bought a musical instrument and lessons, equipment for a sport, golf clubs and lessons, or paid for education at a tech school or college to better prepare them for their future vocation.

An important aspect of release is timing. Because we have practiced for this moment, we can know exactly the time of their release. We can learn from Mary the mother of Jesus. Take notice of how Mary pushed her Son into His time of release.

## PREPARE ME TO LIVE INDEPENDENTLY OF YOU

*John 2:3:* "When the wine ran out, the mother of Jesus said to him, 'They have no wine.' And Jesus said to her, 'Woman, what does this have to do with me? My hour has not yet come.' His mother said to the servants, 'Do whatever he tells you.'"

Jesus did not know it was His time, but Mary did! Some kids are timid or unsure of when they are ready; therefore, as the father, we give them the assurance that it is time for them to be independent and self-supporting.

It is in the heart of every father to prepare his children to impact society and the kingdom of God in a greater measure than he has. We want to transfer generational blessing to the following generations, positioning them to be more effective than the generation that preceded them.

This principle is made clear by the example of the priesthood of Aaron. His priestly garments were soaked with holy anointing oil by Moses at the beginning of his priesthood. Each of his successors would be anointed wearing Aaron's priestly garments—a new anointing each time for service in the same position. I believe that it was God's plan that each generation of the priesthood would have a greater anointing on their lives than the previous one.

The promise and wealth that was given to Abraham has been passed down to each succeeding generation to this time. It will culminate with Messiah's rule in Israel—the Promised Land. He is the God of Abraham, Isaac, Jacob, and all who follow.

Jesus once said to His apostles, "He who believes in Me, the works that I do he will do also; and greater works than these he will do" (John 14:12, NKJV). At first, you might wonder how the apostles could do greater works than what Jesus did. After all, Jesus walked on water, healed lepers, raised the dead, and cast out devils. But Jesus was teaching them that His personal influence was limited to a small area and a small number of people. When He put His

Spirit in them, then His works would be multiplied through His disciples. The apostles would be able to accomplish so much more because they would be able to spread out over the face of the world. And they did!

## Children, Like Arrows, Can Go Where We Cannot

Like arrows, our children can go farther, faster, and more powerfully than we can. I anticipate that whatever I may be able to accomplish in life, my children will do even greater.

May we recognize the incredible responsibility we have of carefully, deliberately, and skillfully shaping them to be used as weapons of war for the advancement of the kingdom of God.

Samuel was sent by God to the house of Jesse to anoint the next king in Israel. As the sons of Jesse passed by, Samuel thought each one had the appearance of a king. After examining the sons of Jesse he never received a confirmation from God that any of them was the one to be anointed king. He then asked Jesse if there was another. Of course there was—it was David, and he became the anointed one.

What a father Jesse must have been, that when the prophet was looking for a king, each of his sons appealed to Samuel as a likely candidate for kingship. We discover that David's three older brothers were present at the battle where the Philistine army and the giant Goliath challenged the army of Israel. It was at this battle that David gained his reputation as a mighty warrior. May our goal be to develop our children with the same appearance and commitment of Jesse's sons.

May our children be blessed by our skillful preparation to help them succeed in life because they were placed in the hands of a warrior.

## PREPARE ME TO LIVE INDEPENDENTLY OF YOU

That day will come when you walk your daughter down the aisle to give her away. It will be the longest walk of your life. Or maybe you'll be sitting beside your wife, watching as your son sees his bride for the first time. Memories will flood your mind, and you will relive your child's life in a few seconds. You will be asking yourself, *Is she ready for this?* or *Did I teach him everything he needs to know to be a good husband?*

The day will come when that young man packs his bags and walks out the door to further his education or step into his destiny. He is now establishing his independence. You will ask yourself, *Have I done all that I could to prepare him for this moment?*

As difficult as it may be to let go of our children, there are some real positive sides to it. If we have prepared them to live life independent from us, the reward will be a sense of accomplishment, completion, and rightness. It is done. Despite the pain of the loss of their presence in the home, there is a deep, underlying sense of relief that we have accomplished our goal. We have prepared them for the time of release. They can live independently of us.

## DISCUSSION QUESTIONS

1. Why are children represented as arrows in Scripture?

2. What are five critical emotional needs of children?

3. Do you know God's purpose for giving your children life? How are you assisting them to hit the target that God has for their future?

4. What does a balanced life avoid?

5. Describe the picture of the person in whose hand God has placed the arrows. Who is holding the arrows?

6. Have you practiced releasing your children? If yes, when and how?

# Conclusion

**M**Y HOPE IS THAT THIS BOOK WILL help the father who reads it to understand the deep desires your children have concerning you. It has also been my intention to help fathers to become better fathers.

Our Heavenly Father has given us a clear example to follow. If we follow His example, we will enjoy fatherhood and will have children who desire to honor us.

The God that our children worship will be the God of their father. Because we are fathers, we represent the fatherhood of God to our children. We are not perfect. We cannot be too harsh with ourselves. Our children may not remember a lot of our teachings, but they will never forget how and if we loved them and desired to fulfill their needs.

If you "so love" them, they will not remember your blunders. They will long embrace the memory of your love.

Though you are a father, you are also a son. Make every attempt to maintain or develop a good relationship with your own father. Your children are watching. And as a dad, may you remove all the barriers that keep your children at a distance, and give them the father they deserve.